DISCIPLE *for* LIFE

D1607019

Knowing Jesus

LIVING BY HIS NAME

- -

Robby Gallaty

LifeWay Press®
Nashville, Tennessee

Published by LifeWay Press® • © 2016 Robby Gallaty

No part of this book may be reproduced or transmitted in any form or by any means, electronic or mechanical, including photocopying and recording, or by any information storage or retrieval system, except as may be expressly permitted in writing by the publisher. Requests for permission should be addressed in writing to LifeWay Press®; One LifeWay Plaza; Nashville, TN 37234-0152.

ISBN 978-1-4300-6394-0 • Item 005791554

Dewey decimal classification: 232.903
Subject headings: JOHN, APOSTLE \ JESUS CHRIST \ CHRISTIAN LIFE

Unless indicated otherwise, Scripture quotations are taken from the Holman Christian Standard Bible®, Copyright © 1999, 2000, 2002, 2003, 2009 by Holman Bible Publishers. Used by permission. Holman Christian Standard Bible®, Holman CSB®, and HCSB® are federally registered trademarks of Holman Bible Publishers. Scripture quotations marked NIV are taken from the Holy Bible, NEW INTERNATIONAL VERSION®. Copyright © 1973, 1978, 1984 by Biblica Inc. All rights reserved worldwide. Used by permission.

To order additional copies of this resource, write to LifeWay Resources Customer Service; One LifeWay Plaza; Nashville, TN 37234-0113; fax 615.251.5933; call toll free 800.458.2772; order online at *lifeway.com;* email *orderentry@lifeway.com;* or visit the LifeWay Christian Store serving you.

Printed in the United States of America

Groups Ministry Publishing • LifeWay Resources • One LifeWay Plaza • Nashville, TN 37234-0152

Contents

About the Author

Robby Gallaty has served as the senior
pastor of Long Hollow Baptist Church
in Hendersonville, Tennessee, since 2015.
He wasn't always a pastor, though.

For three years Robby battled a drug addiction
that ravaged his life. A $180-a-day heroin and
cocaine addiction drove him to steal $15,000 from
his parents. After living without gas, electricity, and water for months;
losing eight of his friends to drug-related deaths; watching six friends get
arrested; and completing two rehabilitation treatments, Robby remembered
the gospel that a friend shared with him in college and was radically saved
on November 12, 2002.

Eight months later David Platt, a seminary student and church member
at the time, asked Robby to meet weekly for accountability, prayer, and
Bible study. For the next two years David instilled a passion for missions,
expository preaching, and disciple making in Robby's life. He also encouraged Robby to go back to school to pursue theological education.

Robby earned his master of divinity in expository preaching in 2007
and his PhD in preaching in 2011 from New Orleans Baptist Theological
Seminary. Today Robby's gospel conviction and evangelistic zeal compel
him to passionately make disciples who make disciples.

In addition to his leadership at Long Hollow, Robby is also the founder
of Replicate Ministries and the author of several books, including *Growing
Up, Firmly Planted,* and *Rediscovering Discipleship.*

Robby and his wife, Kandi, have two young sons: Rig and Ryder.

Introduction

Place yourself in the first century A.D., a few decades after the miraculous resurrection of a controversial Nazarene who claimed to be the Son of God.

Detailed accounts of this man's life and teachings had been circulating for a few decades by this point. Matthew, written by a former tax collector who had spent three years following Him, was filled with details that a Jewish audience would have immediately picked up on. Mark closely followed the actions of Jesus' ministry as He traveled between towns healing, casting out demons, and preaching about the kingdom of God. Luke was a meticulously researched account written by someone who was probably a Gentile doctor and had come to believe in this Jewish man as the Son of God.

So why would another one of Jesus' disciples feel the need, under the inspiration of the Holy Spirit, to write a fourth account?

Even though the word of the gospel had spread far and wide by this point, many people were being taught heretical doctrine. Some had no problem believing Jesus was a good teacher, but they didn't believe He was the Son of God. John wrote his book to examine Jesus' very nature. He intended to bring the focus back onto Jesus Himself, proving that He was both fully man and fully God.

Today we find ourselves in a similar situation, when there are as many opinions about who Jesus was as there are people talking about Him. Now, more than ever, we need to reevaluate the way we look at Jesus. Was He just a good teacher, or was He more?

As we mine the rich theology encased in the Book of John and come to know Jesus, we'll find that the answer to this question will change everything. Our response to it is the most crucial step we'll take in our lives.

How to Use This Study

This Bible study book includes six weeks of content. Each week has an introductory page summarizing the focus of the week's study, followed by content designed for groups and individuals.

GROUP SESSIONS

Regardless of the day of the week your group meets, each week of content begins with the group session. This group session is designed to be one hour or more, with approximately 15 to 20 minutes of teaching and 45 minutes of personal interaction. It's even better if your group is able to meet longer than an hour, allowing more time for participants to interact with one another.

Each group session uses the following format to facilitate simple yet meaningful interaction among group members, with God's Word, and with the video teaching by a group of trusted pastors.

Start

This page includes questions to get the conversation started and to introduce the video segment.

Watch

This page includes key points from the video teaching, along with space for taking notes as participants watch the video.

Discuss

These two pages include questions and statements that guide the group to respond to the video teaching and to relevant Bible passages.

Pray

This final page of each group session includes a prompt for a closing time of prayer together and space for recording prayer requests of group members.

INDIVIDUAL DISCOVERY

Each *Disciple for Life* small-group resource provides individuals with optional activities during the week, appealing to different learning styles, schedules, and levels of engagement. These options include a plan for application and accountability, a Scripture-reading plan with journaling prompts, a devotion, and two personal studies. You can choose to take advantage of some or all of the options provided.

This Week's Plan

Immediately following the group session's prayer page is a weekly plan offering guidance for everyone to engage with that week's focal point, regardless of a person's maturity level or that week's schedule.

Read

A daily reading plan is outlined for Scriptures related to the group session. Space for personal notes is also provided. Instructions for using the HEAR journaling method for reading Scripture can be found on pages 8–11.

Reflect

A one-page devotional option is provided each week to help members reflect on a biblical truth related to the group session.

Personal Study

Two personal studies are provided each week to take individuals deeper into Scripture and to supplement the biblical truths introduced in the teaching time. These pages challenge individuals to grow in their understanding of God's Word and to make practical application to their lives.

LEADER GUIDE

Pages 120–31 at the back of this book contain a guide that develops a leader's understanding of the thought process behind questions and suggests ways to engage members at different levels of life-changing discussion.

The HEAR Journaling Method for Reading Scripture

Daily Bible Reading

Disciple for Life small-group Bible studies include a daily reading plan for each week. Making time in a busy schedule to focus on God through His Word is a vital part of the Christian life. If you're unable to do anything else provided in your Bible study book during a certain week, try to spend a few minutes in God's Word. The verse selections will take you deeper into stories and concepts that support the teaching and discussion during that week's group session.

Why Do You Need a Plan?

When you're a new believer or at various other times in your life, you may find yourself in a place where you don't know where to begin reading your Bible or how to personally approach Scripture. You may have tried the open-and-point method when you simply opened your Bible and pointed to a verse, hoping to get something out of the random selection from God's Word. Reading random Scriptures won't provide solid biblical growth any more then eating random food from your pantry will provide solid physical growth.

An effective plan must be well balanced for healthy growth. When it comes to reading the Bible, *well balanced* and *effective* mean reading and applying. A regular habit is great, but simply checking a box off your task list when you've completed your daily reading isn't enough. Knowing more about God is also great, but simply reading for spiritual knowledge still isn't enough. You also want to respond to what you're reading by taking action as you listen to what God is saying. After all, it's God's Word.

To digest more of the Word, *Disciple for Life* small-group Bible studies not only provide a weekly reading plan but also encourage you to use a simplified version of the HEAR journaling method. (If this method advances your personal growth, check out *Foundations: A 260-Day Bible-Reading Plan for Busy Believers* by Robby and Kandi Gallaty.)

Journaling What You HEAR in God's Word

You may or may not choose to keep a separate journal in addition to the space provided in this book. A separate journal would provide extra space as well as the opportunity to continue your journal after this study is completed. The HEAR journaling method promotes reading the Bible with a life-transforming purpose. You'll read in order to understand and respond to God's Word.

The HEAR acronym stands for *highlight, explain, apply,* and *respond.* Each of these four steps creates an atmosphere for hearing God speak. After settling on a reading plan, like the one provided in this book in the section "Read" each week, establish a time for studying God's Word. Then you'll be ready to HEAR from God.

Before You Begin: The Most Important Step

To really HEAR God speak to you through His Word, always begin your time with prayer. Pause and sincerely ask God to speak to you. It's absolutely imperative that you seek God's guidance in order to understand His Word (see 1 Cor. 2:12-14). Every time you open your Bible, pray a simple prayer like the one David prayed: "Open my eyes so that I may contemplate wonderful things from Your instruction" (Ps. 119:18).

H = Highlight

After praying for the Holy Spirit's guidance, open this book to the week's reading plan, open a journal if you'd like more space than this book provides, and open your Bible. For an illustration let's assume you're reading Philippians 4:10-13. Verse 13 may jump out and speak to you as something you want to remember, so you'd simply highlight that verse in your Bible.

If keeping a HEAR journal, on the top line write the Scripture reference and the date and make up a title to summarize the meaning of the passage. Then write the letter H and record the verse that stood out and that you highlighted in your Bible. This practice will make it easy to look back through your journal to find a passage you want to revisit in the future.

E = Explain

After you've highlighted your verse(s), explain what the text means. Most simply, how would you summarize this passage in your own words? By asking some simple questions, with the help of God's Spirit, you can understand the meaning of the passage or verse. (A good study Bible can help answer more in-depth questions as you learn to explain a passage of Scripture.) Here are a few good questions to get you started:

- Why was the verse or passage written?
- To whom was it originally written?
- How does the verse or passage fit with the verses before and after it?
- Why would the Holy Spirit include this passage in the Bible book?
- What does God intend to communicate through the text?

If keeping a HEAR journal, below the H write the letter E and explain the text in your own words. Record any answers to questions that help you understand the passage of Scripture.

A = Apply

At this point you're beginning the process of discovering the specific personal word God has for you from His Word. What's important is that you're engaging with the text and wrestling with the meaning. Application is the heart of the process. Everything you've done so far coalesces under this heading. As you've done before, answer a series of questions to discover the significance of these verses to you personally, questions like:

- How can this verse or passage help me?
- What's God saying to me?
- What would the application of this verse look like in my life?

These questions bridge the gap between the ancient world and your world today. They provide a way for God to speak to you through the specific passage or verse.

If keeping a HEAR journal, write the letter A under the letter E, where you wrote a short summary explaining the text. Challenge yourself to write between two and five sentences about the way the text applies to your life.

R = Respond

Finally, you'll respond to the text. A personal response may take on many forms. You may write an action step to do, describe a change in perspective, or simply respond in prayer to what you've learned. For example, you may ask for help in being bold or generous, you may need to repent of unconfessed sin, or you may need to praise God. Keep in mind that you're responding to what you've just read.

In this book or in your journal, record your personal application of each passage of Scripture. You may want to write a brief explanation-and-application summary: "The verse means _____ , so I can or will _____."

If keeping a HEAR journal, write the letter R, along with the way you'll respond to what you highlighted, explained, and applied.

Notice that all the words in the HEAR method are action words: *highlight, explain, apply, respond.* God doesn't want us to sit back and wait for Him to drop truth into our laps. God wants us to actively pursue Him instead of waiting passively. Jesus said:

> Keep asking, and it will be given to you. Keep searching, and you
> will find. Keep knocking, and the door will be opened to you.
> **Matthew 7:7**

Revealing His Identity

Week 1

John's Gospel starts as Genesis does: in the beginning.

Creation is the bedrock of a biblical worldview, for it's the first ultimate truth: God made everything. He wove it like fabric. He spun it like clay. He breathed it into formation like glass.

More remarkable than what God did is the way He did it: His tool was His Word. He spoke, and it was. The apostle John traced this Word through time.

Men spoke of this Word while surrounded by both sea and sand, from human thrones and from pits of despair. One man in the wilderness, dressed in leather and camel hair, announced that this Word that gives light to everyone was coming into the world wrapped in human flesh.

A remarkable claim like this requires remarkable evidence, and John provided it for us. In John's Gospel we come to know Jesus in the same way evidence is presented to a jury in a courtroom. John introduced witnesses who testified of the Word made flesh. He examined the words Jesus said about Himself. He described the things Jesus did that testified of His divinity.

Everything you're about to see points to one conclusion: Jesus Christ is the Son of God, and by believing, you can have life through Him.

Start

Welcome to session 1 of *Knowing Jesus*. Use the following content to begin your group session together.

We've become experts at filling every hour of our days with something—work, recreation, friends, family, school, church, and daily routines. We have email, text, Internet, and even live chat at our fingertips 24-7. We have smartphones with as many apps as they can hold; inexpensive video-streaming accounts; and endless hours of books, blogs, and games to consume. We squeeze in time between meetings or shifts to check off items on to-do lists or to catch up with activity in our social-media feeds.

What unavoidable responsibilities fill your day?

What additional things do you add to your day?

How do you relax and recharge after a long day?

We first encounter Jesus after He and His disciples had had a trying day. They started out with a long boat ride across the Sea of Tiberias. A large crowd of people immediately flocked to them, attracted by the One they had seen work miracles. The disciples worked during Jesus' all-day healing and teaching service, were directed to distribute food for dinner, and then had to pick up all the leftovers. It had been a long day; all they wanted was to get back to their boat, row home, and sleep. As it turns out, their long day was about to get longer.

Pray that God will open your hearts and minds as you watch video session 1.

Watch

The more we know Jesus, the more we _____ Him. The more
we love Him, the more we _____ Him. The more we obey Him,
the more He _____ Himself to us.

Jesus is always _____, spending time with the Father.

Jesus discloses His _____ in an amazing way.

What Jesus is saying, without saying anything, is that He is _____.

Jesus _____ _____ by saying, "Don't be afraid."

_____ _____ is the verb *to be*. God always is, He always was,
and He always will be. He's always in the eternal present.

Discuss

Use the following statements and questions to discuss the video.

The opening of the video included the following statement about Jesus:

> The more we know Him, the more we love Him. The more we love Him, the more we obey Him. The more we obey Him, the more He manifests Himself.

How does this cyclical process help you understand discipleship?

Read Mark 6:47-50 and John 6:16-20.

In John's account what physical details in each verse help set the emotional tone?

What additional details did Mark include? How do they add to the intensity of the situation?

What did Jesus do while the disciples were struggling against the wind?

Robby pointed out that this situation was the second time Jesus took something the disciples knew well—the lake—and used it to teach them dependence on Him.

How does adversity help us learn dependence?

What was something significant Robby pointed out in Mark 6:48?

The accounts of Jesus walking on the water contained proof of Jesus' divinity: the fact that He walked on the waves (see Job 9:8) and His response to the disciples' fear.

How did Jesus respond when He saw that the disciples were afraid? What was significant about the way He referred to Himself?

In what situations have you felt that you were struggling in the dark, needing to hear Jesus say, "Fear not, for I AM"?

Read Matthew 14:27-33.

Matthew's account gives further insight into the events of that evening, particularly Peter's involvement. But it also shows us something important that happened after Jesus got into the boat.

How did the disciples respond to what Jesus performed that evening on the lake?

What proof do you think convinced them?

If you've reached the same conclusion the disciples did in Matthew 14:33, what convinced you? If you haven't, what do you think it would take?

Before we transition to prayer, something we'll do at the end of each group session, think about what we saw before Jesus walked on the water. Jesus intentionally took time at the end of a long day to go off by Himself to pray. We don't often think of Jesus as needing to rest and be refreshed. While we don't know exactly what He was praying in this instance, we see an invaluable example for our relationship with God.

How does prayer refresh you? How does it keep you focused on God instead of fearful of your circumstances?

What's your most difficult challenge to a consistent, healthy prayer life?

Conclude the group session with the prayer activity on the following page.

Pray

We, like the disciples, tend to get terrified when things around us seem as if they're falling apart. We may have moments of boldness, but they often become moments of doubt. Whether or not we admit it, we look for a Savior to come walking on the water to rescue us. Jesus did just that, and He used the disciples' struggle to teach them a lesson.

> Spend a few minutes sharing with the group situations—whether personal circumstances, world events, or friends' experiences—that seem beyond hope or control.

> Read aloud Matthew 8:23-27. Close by thanking God for His sovereign control, praying that He will help us see Him for who He is and worship Him appropriately.

Prayer Requests

Encourage members to complete "This Week's Plan" before the next group session.

This Week's Plan

In addition to studying God's Word, work with your group leader to create a plan for personal study, worship, and application between now and the next session. Select from the following optional activities to match your personal preferences and available time.

Worship

[ ] Read your Bible. This Bible study book will help you read the Gospel of John over the next six weeks. Complete the reading plan on page 20.

[ ] Spend time with God by engaging with the devotional experience on page 21.

[ ] Connect with God each day through prayer.

Personal Study

[ ] Read and interact with "A Man Born Blind" on page 22.

[ ] Read and interact with "A Man Brought Back" on page 26.

Application

[ ] Spend time in personal reflection, looking for signs of a coming storm on your horizon. Consider ways you can prepare ahead of time to keep your eyes focused on Jesus, no matter what happens.

[ ] Memorize John 6:20.

[ ] Pray for an opportunity to share your testimony with someone outside the group this week. If you know somebody who's experiencing something you've been through, pray for an opportunity to encourage that person.

[ ] Start a journal. This week write about a time you've tried to brave a storm on your own and describe the way it turned out. Journal about a time you've trusted your situation entirely to God and describe the way it turned out.

[ ] Other:

Did you miss the group session?
Video sessions available for purchase at *LifeWay.com/KnowingJesus*

19

Read

Read the following Scripture passages this week. Use the acronym HEAR and the space provided to record your thoughts or action steps.

Day 1: John 1:1-28

Day 2: John 1:29-51

Day 3: John 2:1-12

Day 4: John 2:13-25

Day 5: John 3:1-21

Day 6: John 3:22-36

Day 7: John 4

HIGHLIGHT • EXPLAIN • APPLY • RESPOND

Reflect

CERTAINTY OF THE UNSEEN

Has this thought ever crossed your mind? *If I had been in that boat with the disciples, I would have believed too.* It's so much easier to trust Jesus when you can see Him walking on the waves toward you with your own eyes. We're good at feeling the pressure from the wind and the swell of the waves underneath our boats. We can hear our planks creaking and see our masts swaying too heavily. It's harder to trust Jesus, whom we can't see.

Consider what the writer of Hebrews said about faith without sight:

> Faith is the reality of what is hoped for, the proof of what is not seen.
> **Hebrews 11:1**

The author of Hebrews tells us that faith isn't what we have in spite of a lack of evidence. Faith is what we have in lieu of needing evidence at all. Our faith is our evidence. People who are called by Jesus' name have experienced His saving grace at some point. They're filled with the Holy Spirit, who guides, corrects, and counsels them. They're driven by a thirst for the Word of God.

When faith seems hard, remember that you can still see Him; you can see Him at work in your life. You can still hear Him; you can hear His voice through His Word. "Those who believe without seeing are blessed" (John 20:29), Jesus said.

Identify ways Jesus has revealed Himself to you. These reminders will comfort you when the storm comes.

Personal Study 1

A MAN BORN BLIND

Everything John included in his Gospel has a point: to prove that Jesus is who He said He was. So occasionally, John described instances when Jesus was on trial in a manner of speaking. One such occasion is in John 9. Let's examine the evidence John provided.

Read John 9.

Rabbis claimed only the Son of God could do certain things. Healing a man born blind and raising a man from death to life were two of them. Those seem like fair expectations. Not much argument there, right?

John 9:I, written to an audience who understood this, established the stakes right off the bat.

The disciples tried to rationalize the man's condition by asking why he was born this way. Jesus gave them an answer they probably didn't expect: so that His glory could be shown.

> **What's a bad incident that happened in your life that doesn't have a rational explanation?**

> **How did you get through it?**

How can Jesus be magnified through a person's response to devastating circumstances in his or her life?

As soon as the man came home seeing, it absolutely shook things up. His eyes, which had previously seen only darkness, now let light in.

Verses 8-12 show that the gravity of this situation didn't go unnoticed. The man's neighbors and friends were sincerely baffled by the extraordinary thing that had been done. What was perhaps frustrating to the healed man was that after he went and washed, Jesus wasn't standing there to greet him.

Jesus was doing something incredible: He was letting the healing speak for itself, because He knew what kind of a stir it would cause. The investigation that followed was going to point to Him and come to one of two conclusions: either this man had been lying the whole time about being blind, or Jesus did something that only the Messiah could have done.

Perhaps you've felt the immeasurable peace only Jesus can bring in the face of sadness. Maybe you've felt the crushing weight of your sin lifted.

What's something Jesus has done in your life that can be explained only by Him?

The people instantly knew this was a matter that needed to be investigated. So they took the man to the religious leaders in town—the ones who knew exactly what to look for in the coming Messiah.

So in John 9:13-34 they interviewed everybody who knew this man to figure out whether his story was true. Was he really blind from birth? He wasn't *really* born that way; he did something very, very early that made him blind, didn't he? What exactly did this man do to heal you?

Their questions were insensitive and maddening, especially to the man who was healed. But we find the same things being asked today about the works of God.

What are excuses people make to explain away the work of God?

What has someone said that caused you to doubt your belief in God?

In verses 35-41 Jesus revealed Himself to both the man He healed and the people seeking to inspire doubt about Him. The man's simple profession in verse 38 is contrasted heavily with the angry skepticism coming from the Pharisees:

"I believe, Lord!" he said, and he worshiped Him.
John 9:38

The man's statement set up a grand reversal. The man who was blind could now see, both physically and spiritually. Those who could physically see were made spiritually blind by the healing.

What does it mean to be spiritually blind?

How can the works of God make the blind see and cause the seeing to go blind to His ways?

How can your eyes be opened to see God in all His incredible ways?

Close your study time in prayer, thanking God for all He has done. Pray that your eyes, like those of the man born blind, will be opened to see who Jesus is.

Personal Study 2

A MAN BROUGHT BACK

In personal study 1 you explored John's account of Jesus healing the blind man. Rabbis knew that only God could perform such a miracle. Another thing rabbis knew only the Son of God could do was raise a man from the dead. The logic was perfect: if God is the ultimate giver of life, then giving it again to someone who died is possible.

Just as Jesus did something in John 9 that proved who He was, He used a situation in John 11 to reveal who He was in all His glory.

Read John 11:1-11.

The account of Jesus raising Lazarus from the dead may be a familiar one, but even if you've heard it many times before, let's read it with first-century eyes. As the text points out, Jesus learned of Lazarus's sickness before he died. Mary and Martha knew Jesus, a miraculous healer, could save him if He got there in time, but Jesus did something that probably frustrated them: He waited two extra days before making His way to Lazarus.

When have you asked for God to come and do something like heal a sickness?

What goes through your head when it seems that God isn't acting?

Why do you think Jesus delayed going to save Lazarus?

How do Jesus' words in verse 4 address our desire to see God work on our timetable?

Read John 11:17-27.

John was still presenting a case for people to believe in Jesus, which is made starkly evident in verse 17. Jewish tradition believed a person's spirit hovered around the body for three days after death. If Lazarus had gotten up just a day after they thought he was dead, his resurrection would have been attributed to a misdiagnosis or a false report of his death.

But Lazarus has been dead for four days by this point. Everyone around him knew there was no chance of his coming back. Still, Martha clung to her hope that Jesus could fix it.

Jesus told Martha that Lazarus would rise again, but she thought He was talking about spiritual things. Little did she know that He had plans that would astound her and would prove her incredible confession in verse 27.

Jesus said He's the resurrection and the life (see v. 25). What does this declaration mean to you personally?

What did Jesus mean when He said those who live and believe in Him "will never die—ever" (v. 26)?

Read John 11:38-44.

Something purely unexplainable by human reason happened that day in Bethany. Jesus called out to an open grave filled by the stench of death and an air of hopelessness, and the man who was lying there got up and walked out of it.

More interesting is the reason Jesus said He raised Lazarus. Verse 42 informs us that it was for the benefit of the people looking on.

We're still looking at this resurrection thousands of years after it happened. It happened for us as much as it did for the disciples and Martha. For those of us who've found new life in Christ, what happened to Lazarus actually happened to us as well.

Scripture tells us that we were dead in our sin but were made alive together with Christ—just as Lazarus was.

Read Ephesians 2:1-5.

Describe your life before you came to know Christ.

What was the situation that brought you to a saving knowledge of Jesus?

How has a relationship with Christ changed your perspective on everything around you?

What does a person have to fear who was once dead but was brought back to life to live solely for the One who gave it?

How do your everyday actions change, knowing your life is a gift from God?

Close your study time in prayer, praising God as the One who gives life. Die again to self, firmly placing Jesus at the center of your actions, thoughts, and motivations.

The Power of Faith

Week 2

We learned last week that John's Gospel was written to prove that Jesus is the Messiah. Each week of this Bible study was specifically developed to prove Jesus' identity to you, whether it's by the language John employed or by the words of a witness he recorded.

By the time of the events of today's passage, Jesus had already called five disciples: Andrew, Peter, Philip, Nathanael, and John. This group had been to a wedding party (see John 2:2), had taken a trip to Capernaum for a few days (see 2:12), attended Passover in Jerusalem (see 2:13), met with a religious leader (see 3:1-2), journeyed into the Judean countryside (see 3:22), and taken a short-term mission trip to Samaria (see 4:4).

Jesus' ministry had been eventful too. He had already begun making a name for Himself as a miracle worker, a teacher with authority, and the Savior of the world.

Jesus had become famous enough that an official in Herod's court was unafraid to approach Him in the middle of the day to ask Him an important question.

Start

Welcome everyone to session 2 of *Knowing Jesus*. Use the following content to begin your group session together.

At the end of group session 1, you were asked to identify areas of your life that are out of your control.

> **What's your typical response when you recognize that things are out of your control? Fear? Relief? Other?**

> **Were there specific moments this week when you felt out of control? If so, what were they, and how did you respond?**

> **How does seeing Jesus as the Messiah affect your ideas about control?**

> **What was most insightful or meaningful to you this past week in your reading, journaling, or personal study?**

Last week we explored the incredible truth that Jesus is who He says He is. That's the greatest realization in the world because the way we see Jesus fundamentally changes the way we live our lives.

After seeing Christ for who He is, we begin dealing with this issue called faith. Today we'll see a Jewish official demonstrate what faith looks like, and then we'll take some steps to see just how drastically that kind of faith can affect our lives today.

Pray that God will open your hearts and minds as you watch video session 2.

Watch

Faith is believing and having confidence that God's word is _____ and understanding that when you act upon that faith, it brings God's _____.

Faith is founded upon the _____ of God.

Faith in God is always expressed in _____.

The opposite of faith is not _____. The opposite of faith is _____.

Faith is not just believing in spite of _____. Faith is obeying in spite of the _____.

God's divine instrument for conforming us to the image of Jesus is _____ and _____.

Trials are used by God not to make us _____. God uses trials in our life to make us _____.

Discuss

Use the following statements and questions to discuss the video.

Robby said *faith* can be defined as *believing and having confidence that God's word is true and understanding that when you act upon that faith, it brings God's blessing.*

How is this definition encouraging or helpful? How is it convicting?

Read John 4:43-48.

Why would it have been difficult for the people in Jesus' hometown to recognize His holy identity and divine authority?

In what ways was the royal official in Cana a stark contrast to the people in Jesus' hometown?

Why is it important for us to know that this man held a position of royal authority?

Robby said the opposite of faith isn't unbelief but disobedience.

Was that surprising? Explain your reaction to that statement.

What are some ways you hear from the Lord in order to receive His instruction?

Read John 4:49-54.

Even though the official might not have gotten the response he had antic-ipated from Jesus, his faith wasn't shaken. Knowing Jesus was capable of healing his son, he punctuated the intent of his question with an urgent plea: "Come down before my boy dies!" (v. 49). This man was desperate, and he knew the only One who could heal his son was Jesus.

Why is suffering so effective in revealing the object of our faith?

How has God used suffering in your life to strengthen your faith?

Read James 2:14-19.

Jesus' brother, James, wrote that if faith isn't accompanied by action, it's dead.

On a scale of 1 to 10, 1 being dead and 10 being vibrant, how would you rate your faith? Explain your answer.

How does seeing the official's faith make you feel about your own faith in Jesus Christ? Explain your answer.

If someone looked at your life, how would they describe your faith?

It's sometimes hard for us to separate the ideas of belief and faith. While we can easily say, "I believe Jesus is Lord," acting on it is a little harder. If we truly believe Jesus is the Son of God, that understanding will be visibly demonstrated in the way we live our lives.

What's an example of something you believe to be true about God yet have a hard time putting into action?

How has God shown Himself to be trustworthy when you've demonstrated your faith in Him?

Conclude this session with the prayer activity on the following page.

Pray

Each one of us has experienced suffering in our lives. But as we learned in the video session, affliction is God's way of getting our attention. It's His most effective way of getting us to recognize our need for Him and His strength.

> Spend a few minutes as a group identifying struggles you're going through, whether they seem big or small.

> Read aloud the following passage. Close by praying for open eyes to see suffering the way God wants us to see it. Pray that our suffering will lead us to acknowledge our dependence on Jesus.

> Consider it a great joy, my brothers, whenever you experience various trials, knowing that the testing of your faith produces endurance.
> **James 1:2-3**

> **Prayer Requests**

Encourage members to complete "This Week's Plan" before the next group session.

This Week's Plan

In addition to studying God's Word, work with your group leader to create a plan for personal study, worship, and application between now and the next session. Select from the following optional activities to match your personal preferences and available time.

Worship

[ ] Read your Bible. Complete the reading plan on page 38.

[ ] Spend time with God by engaging with the devotional experience on page 39.

[ ] Connect with God each day through prayer.

Personal Study

[ ] Read and interact with "Practicing Faith" on page 40.

[ ] Read and interact with "Provision of Faith" on page 44.

Application

[ ] Memorize James 1:2-3.

[ ] Continue writing in your journal by making a list of trials you've experienced and the ways you saw God resolve them for His glory.

[ ] Get together with someone from your group this week. Ask the person two things: (1) What's something you're struggling with that you would feel comfortable sharing with me? (2) How can I pray for you or hold you accountable in that challenging situation?

[ ] Other:

Did you miss the group session?
Video sessions available for purchase at *LifeWay.com/KnowingJesus*

37

Read

Read the following Scripture passages this week. Use the acronym HEAR and the space provided to record your thoughts or action steps.

Day 1: John 5:1-30

Day 2: John 5:31-47

Day 3: John 6:1-21

Day 4: John 6:22-59

Day 5: John 6:60–7:9

Day 6: John 7:10-24

Day 7: John 7:25-52

HIGHLIGHT • EXPLAIN • APPLY • RESPOND

Reflect

ULTIMATE AUTHORITY

When we're discussing something important, we're quick to appeal to an authority figure who backs up our opinion. If we were speaking about asteroids, we would want to reference the thoughts of a NASA scientist. If we were discussing literary themes in *Macbeth,* we would probably quote an English professor. However, notice what Mark wrote about Jesus' teaching:

> They [Jesus and the disciples] went into Capernaum, and right
> away He entered the synagogue on the Sabbath and began
> to teach. They were astonished at His teaching because, unlike
> the scribes, He was teaching them as one having authority.
> **Mark 1:21-22**

It was conventional for scribes to appeal to previous writers and traditions when discussing the Torah—so conventional that people were astonished because Jesus never did this. He didn't have to appeal to an authority on Scripture, for He *was* that authority. He didn't have to quote someone's writing about the Word of God, for He *was* the Word of God.

We have the enormous privilege of studying this same Word of God today, and the Word is just as active in your living room as it was when Jesus was reading aloud in a first-century synagogue on the Sabbath. As we dig into the Word, pray that Jesus will instill it in your heart with the same authority that caused all the scribes in the synagogue to hold Him in awe.

How have you heard from God through His Word lately?
What's Jesus teaching you through the words of Scripture?

Personal Study 1

PRACTICING FAITH

First-century Jews found themselves mixed up in a lot of different super-
stitions. One of the more interesting ones is mentioned in John 5:1-15.
The events described in this passage took place at a pool beside one
of Jerusalem's entrances, called the pool of Bethesda.

Here's what the Jews believed about this pool. Every now and again, an
angel would come and stir it up, making it bubble. When the pool started
bubbling, the first person to touch the water would be healed from his
or her affliction. For this reason a number of chronically sick and injured
people would lie around the pool day after day and wait for the bubbles
to come, in hopes they could be the first one to get in.

In Jesus' day one man was well known in the company of those who sat
around the pool. He was sick and couldn't get around very well, but he was
probably famous for one thing: he'd been lying there for 38 years, unable
to get to the healing waters first.

We don't know what the man's actual sickness was. What we do know is
that he lived a relatively simple life, especially compared to those who car-
ried their everyday burdens in the outside world. He had to beg for money,
sure, but his life was most likely a relatively comfortable one. Being healed
would mean leaving that comfort behind.

How have you, like this man, sought comfort in your everyday life?

One day this man was lying by the pool on the Sabbath and a Galilean rabbi singled him out amid all the blind, lame, paralyzed, and ill people waiting for the water to bubble up. He asked the man a strange question: "Do you want to get well?" (v. 6).

Put yourself in this man's position. He was lying near the pool but was making no effort to get in. When have you grown accustomed to and accepting of a circumstance in your life, even though you believed a possible solution was in reach?

If Jesus walked up to you and asked you the same question, what would He know you need to be healed from?

John 5:7 records the man's answer:

"Sir," the sick man answered, "I don't have a man to put me into the pool when the water is stirred up, but while I'm coming, someone goes down ahead of me."
John 5:7

While this man genuinely couldn't have healed himself, he also showed no effort to get into the pool that many believed could heal him. And he didn't reply, "Yes!" to Jesus' question.

When have you given up hope that your circumstance would actually change?

What excuses have you made for a lack of effort to change?

The sick man dodged the question, but that didn't matter to Jesus. Jesus simply replied, "Get up, . . . pick up your mat and walk!" (v. 8).

What would you have to give up for Jesus to heal you from an area of brokenness with which you've become comfortable?

In what ways would walking after lying down for so long require you to have faith in the One who made you well?

It's no accident that living a godly life is compared to a walk. Adam and Eve walked with God in the garden (see Gen. 3:8). Enoch walked with God and then was no more (see Gen. 5:24). Psalm 1 warns against walking in the path of the ungodly. Jesus calls us to die to ourselves, take up our crosses, and follow Him (see Matt. 16:24).

Walking by faith requires leaving things behind, but it also requires putting your trust in the places where you put your feet. If Jesus is the One you're following, it's because you've heard His call to you: "Follow Me."

How does it make you feel to know that your ability to walk by faith comes from Jesus' divine authority and His command to get up and walk?

It's hard to leave the things behind that you're used to, but Jesus was prepared for that. As you'll see in the next personal study with the bread and the fish in John 6:1-13, Jesus is willing and able to satisfy all our needs. If there are things in your life you need to leave behind in order to follow Him, remember that He knew exactly what He was inviting you into when He gave that personal, radical charge: "Follow Me."

Close your study time in prayer, thanking God for taking the initiative to heal your brokenness. Ask Him for faith to walk with Jesus every day.

Personal Study 2

PROVISION OF FAITH

We learned in this week's group session about God's allowance of suffering to draw us nearer to Him. This concept is perfectly easy to understand when you aren't facing suffering. When that situation hits you like a slap in the face, however, it's easy to lose sight of who's in control.

That's OK. Here's the phenomenal thing about Christ: He knows we're prone to divert our attention from His face. He has also promised to be the only source of salvation and true nourishment for our souls.

In John 6:1-13 Jesus provided lunch, with a few loaves of bread and some fish, for what may have been upwards of 15,000 people, including women and children. This incident is truly bizarre and unexplainable, to the point that Jesus' disciples were left scratching their heads. It shows us, however, why someone can say they're able to be content in any situation they find themselves facing: they understand where their sufficiency comes from. Each believer must come to understand who provides the things they need.

How has the Lord provided for you in the past?

The feeding of this multitude is the only miracle besides the resurrection that's included in all four Gospel accounts. As verse 14 tells us, what Jesus did on this mountainside was enough to prove to the people that He was the Messiah they had been waiting for. The reason? He came out and told them—but as an Eastern rabbi, not as a Western pastor.

In Deuteronomy the Lord told Moses what the people should be looking for in the Messiah:

> … a prophet like you from among their brothers. I will put My words
> in his mouth, and he will tell them everything I command him.
> **Deuteronomy 18:18**

As Jesus showed the people connection after connection between Himself and the prophets in the Old Testament, some came to understand that He was the One they were looking for.

This instance of feeding the multitude was not only practical but also incredibly symbolic. It was a sign pointing to His identity as the promised Messiah who would save God's people. Shockingly, even after such an amazing miracle, people were still asking what Jesus would do to prove that He was the fulfillment of prophecy.

Read the following passage, paying attention to the images used:

> "What sign then are You going to do so we may see and believe You?" they
> asked. "What are You going to perform? Our fathers ate the manna in the
> wilderness, just as it is written: He gave them bread from heaven to eat."
>   Jesus said to them, "I assure you: Moses didn't give you the bread from
> heaven, but My Father gives you the real bread from heaven. For the bread
> of God is the One who comes down from heaven and gives life to the world."
>   Then they said, "Sir, give us this bread always!"
> **John 6:30-34**

The Jews asked for a sign like the one God gave to the Israelites in the wilderness. When do you find yourself asking God for a sign?

Not a lot has changed between the first century and today. We're still people who ask for signs. But when the people asked Jesus for a sign, He didn't stand before them and perform a miracle. Instead, He answered them simply:

> "I am the bread of life," Jesus told them. "No one who comes to Me will ever be hungry, and no one who believes in Me will ever be thirsty again. But as I told you, you've seen Me, and yet you do not believe. Everyone the Father gives Me will come to Me, and the one who comes to Me I will never cast out. For I have come down from heaven, not to do My will, but the will of Him who sent Me. This is the will of Him who sent Me: that I should lose none of those He has given Me but should raise them up on the last day. For this is the will of My Father: that everyone who sees the Son and believes in Him may have eternal life, and I will raise him up on the last day."
> **John 6:35-40**

When the people asked Jesus for a sign, He simply pointed to Himself. He used the image they began, of the manna from heaven, but instead of working another spectacular wonder, He connected the bread from heaven directly to Himself.

Jesus used the image of bread to show that He's our source of life. What images from your daily life would you use to describe Jesus' identity?

What tangible needs has Jesus met in your life?

What hunger inside you has Jesus filled?

Just as Jesus met the Israelites where they were, using the language they used, addressing the specific need they had, He's more than capable of meeting you where you are so that you can personally find your fulfillment in Him.

Use the space below to make a list of needs in your life—tangible matters of provision or intangible matters of your heart and mind. Nothing is too big or too small to bring before God in prayer.

Close your time in prayer. Present your needs to God and thank Him for perfectly filling the hunger in your heart.

Spiritual Growth

Week 3

It takes years to produce a single grape that's edible. In fact, if a vinedresser is going to plant a vineyard, he's supposed to prohibit the tree from bearing any fruit at all for a few years. While this strategy is disheartening and may seem unfair, the reason is simple. The roots of a young grapevine aren't strong enough to support the weight of the fruit until it has been seasoned for a while.

Growing grapes was common knowledge in the first century, particularly in Israel. For generations Scripture compared Israel to a grapevine, and God was the Vinedresser.

But one fact stands out as we look at the history of Israel. They were more often than not a bad vine. The fact that they were God's chosen people didn't stop them from living in almost constant rebellion. It got so bad that God ceased giving them His Word for hundreds of years until one miraculous day when He sent His Word in the flesh to walk among us.

Start

Welcome to session 3 of *Knowing Jesus*. Use the following content to begin your group session together.

In the previous group session you were asked to name current struggles you're facing, no matter how big or small they seem.

> **As you spent time in God's Word this week, how did your faith in Christ grow?**

> **How did your faith in who Jesus is change the way you view your struggles?**

> **How have you been comforted by knowing that Jesus promised to be all the sufficiency you need to follow Him?**

> **What else was meaningful to you this past week in your reading, journaling, or personal study? Why?**

In this session we'll see that once we're rooted in Christ, He uses two methods to make sure we're growing properly: pruning and purging. In today's video session Robby shows that Jesus is the True Vine and reveals how we're to grow in Him.

Pray that God will open your hearts and minds as you watch video session 3.

Watch

God takes away anything that doesn't accomplish the most _____
in our lives.

The Difference Between Pruning and Disciplining

Pruning is for when you see _____.

Discipline is for when you see _____.

Both are equally _____, but they are for a different _____.

The more you abide, the more you desire to _____. The more
you pray, the more you want to _____.

The _____ Jesus got, the more He _____.

Discuss

Use the following statements and questions to discuss the video.

Robby began this session by saying that Jesus' statement "I am the true vine" (John 15:1) means He's the source of everything we need.

Read aloud John 15:1-8.

> **Based on what we've learned during the past week and in today's session, in what ways is Christ all-sufficient as the source of the Christian life?**

Jesus removed the burden from our shoulders by calling Himself the True Vine. It isn't up to us to water ourselves; that's for the Vinedresser to do. It isn't up to us to be planted in the ground, for that's what Jesus does. We're only branches on His vine, though with that come some harsh realities.

> **What's the difference between pruning and purging?**

Jesus said God prunes branches that produce fruit so that they can produce more fruit.

> **What are examples of losing something that results in a healthier and stronger faith?**

Jesus also said whatever doesn't remain in Him is thrown away and burned.

> **How can you recognize whether something in your life needs purging?**

Robby pointed out the while there are different purposes, pruning and purging may be equally painful in the moment.

> **When have you experienced a painful season that you later recognized as pruning that resulted in fresh growth in your life?**

What fruit have you seen from the pain and growth of pruning?

The sooner we realize that our source in the Christian life is Jesus Christ, the sooner we'll bear His fruit. To understand how to remain rooted in God, Robby pointed out what Jesus did: He lived a prayerful life.

The busier Jesus was, the more He prayed.

How often do you excuse your lack of prayer, time alone with God, or worshiping Him because you're too busy?

Mark 1:35 reads:

> Very early in the morning, while it was still dark, [Jesus] got up, went
> out, and made His way to a deserted place. And He was praying there.
> **Mark 1:35**

Even on the heels of a long day and at the start of another one, Jesus made an extra effort to be alone with His Father.

When do you spend time alone with the Father?

What kinds of things do you pray for?

When do you find yourself praying most often?

We're a busier society than perhaps any that has come before us, but the way we remain in Christ is to constantly connect with Him through prayer.

What areas of your life do you need to rearrange in order to spend more time with God?

Conclude the group session with the prayer activity on the following page.

Pray

Many Christians seem all too eager to break out of the world to get to heaven. What Scripture reveals is the opposite. God is a coming-down God.

- God came down and walked with Adam in the garden.

- God came down and made His residence in the camp of His people.

- God came down and guided His people out of captivity.

- God came down and met with Moses on top of a mountain.

- God came down and gave His word to the prophets.

- God came down and wrapped Himself in flesh to dwell among us and to die for us.

Respond either individually or as a group to this question:

How do you experience this coming-down God in your life today?

Take a moment to make a list of distractions that keep you from seeing God. Then take prayer requests and spend a few minutes in prayer to your Heavenly Father.

Prayer Requests

Encourage members to complete "This Week's Plan" before the next group session.

This Week's Plan

In addition to studying God's Word, work with your group leader to create a plan for personal study, worship, and application between now and the next session. Select from the following optional activities to match your personal preferences and available time.

Worship

[ ] Read your Bible. Complete the reading plan on page 56.

[ ] Spend time with God by engaging with the devotional experience on page 57.

[ ] Connect with God each day through prayer.

Personal Study

[ ] Read and interact with "Abide in the Truth" on page 58.

[ ] Read and interact with "Christ Is All-Sufficient" on page 62.

Application

[ ] Set your alarm 30 minutes earlier each day this week. Try out a scheduled, intentional prayer time and note ways it changes you by the time of your next group session.

[ ] Memorize John 15:7-8.

[ ] Reach out to someone you haven't talked to in a while and spend time listening to them and hearing how they're doing. Look for opportunities to encourage them to abide in Christ.

[ ] Other:

Did you miss the group session?
Video sessions available for purchase at *LifeWay.com/KnowingJesus*

55

Read

Read the following Scripture passages this week. Use the acronym HEAR and the space provided to record your thoughts or action steps.

Day 1: John 8:1-11

Day 2: John 8:12-30

Day 3: John 8:31-59

Day 4: John 9:1-12

Day 5: John 9:13-27

Day 6: John 9:28-41

Day 7: John 10:1-21

HIGHLIGHT • EXPLAIN • APPLY • RESPOND

Reflect

ASK FOR WHATEVER YOU WANT

One of the most important people on a movie set is the first assistant camera. His purpose is to keep the subject in focus. A number of things can be fixed after a scene is shot, but if the shot isn't perfectly focused at all times, nothing can be done to salvage it. That footage is unusable.

In John 15:7 Jesus tells us something interesting:

> If you remain in Me and My words remain in you,
> ask whatever you want and it will be done for you.
> **John 15:7**

Jesus was saying something both simple and profound: "Make My wants your wants, and then ask for whatever you want." When our focus is on Christ, it fundamentally changes how we see, what we search for, and where our hope lies.

The hymn "Turn Your Eyes upon Jesus" captures Jesus' words like this:

> Turn your eyes upon Jesus,
> Look full in His wonderful face,
> And the things of earth will grow strangely dim
> In the light of His glory and grace.[1]

The more we see of Christ, the more we become like Him. The more we become like Him, the more of His desires we'll have. And because Jesus is God, who works all things according to His will, we can safely ask for the things He wants and see them come to fruition.

---

1. Helen H. Lemmel, "Turn Your Eyes upon Jesus," in *Baptist Hymnal* (Nashville: LifeWay Worship, 2008), 413.

Personal Study 1

ABIDE IN THE TRUTH

Here's a simple question: Why did Jesus come into the world?

Ask this question of most people in the church, and they'll likely give a similar answer: to die for our sins, to repair the damage done by humans in their relationship with God, to seek and to save the lost, and so on. These are all good biblical answers, and they're all things Jesus did, but they don't express the reason He came.

Read John 18:37-38.

> "You are a king then?" Pilate asked.
> "You say that I'm a king," Jesus replied. "I was born for this, and I have come into the world for this: to testify to the truth. Everyone who is of the truth listens to My voice."
> "What is truth?" said Pilate.
> **John 18:37-38**

What are some ways people determine what they believe to be true?

We live in a society that wants to make Truth lowercase. They want to say, "Truth is what's true for me, and that's all that matters."

Why is making truth a purely personal matter dangerous?

What happens if two people's "truths" collide with each other?

What did Jesus mean when He said He came "to testify to the truth" (v. 37)? Where does that mean truth actually resides?

Read John 8:31-36.

> Jesus said to the Jews who had believed Him, "If you continue in My word, you really are My disciples. You will know the truth, and the truth will set you free."
>
> "We are descendants of Abraham," they answered Him, "and we have never been enslaved to anyone. How can You say, 'You will become free'?"
>
> Jesus responded, "I assure you: Everyone who commits sin is a slave of sin. A slave does not remain in the household forever, but a son does remain forever. Therefore, if the Son sets you free, you really will be free."
> **John 8:31-36**

How would you define *freedom?*

Why is sin the opposite of freedom? How does sin enslave you?

Sin isn't something we have to learn; it's engrained in us from the moment we're born. We sin because we're sinners. Sin creates desires in us that threaten to master us. It compels us to elevate our desires above our need for God, and it drives us to a sure end: death.

How does the work of Christ free us from this bondage to sin?

How does submission to Christ liberate us from the driving need to indulge our every desire?

How does Jesus say in John 8:31-36 that we become His disciples?

The word translated as *remain, continue,* or *abide* in John 8:31 is the same word Jesus repeatedly used in John 15. As we abide in His Word, we learn to follow Him more closely. As we learn to follow Him better, we give ourselves over to His lordship instead of sin's domination. As we submit to His lordship, we find ourselves drawn even deeper into His Word.

Abiding in the truth of Christ means dwelling in it day in and day out, as the psalmist wrote:

> His delight is in the LORD's instruction,
> and he meditates on it day and night.
> **Psalm 1:2**

From what bondage do you need to be released by Jesus' power?

As you close your study session, thank God that He provided His Word so that you can know that Truth is a Person, Jesus. Pray that your desire for Him grows every day.

Personal Study 2

CHRIST IS ALL-SUFFICIENT

We live in a time when everything from television commercials to the magazines at the grocery-store checkout counter give advice on how we're supposed to live if we want to be fulfilled.

- We have to lose that extra five pounds.

- We have to buy that brand of clothing.

- We have to see that movie when it comes out.

- We have to meet that perfect someone and fall in love.

- We have to have that perfect house.

   How can you tell the difference between your wants and your needs? Give examples of each.

   What things do you find yourself wanting the most?

Other than Jesus, what's the deepest and most specific need
of your heart right now?

In John 6 you read about two incredible miracles: the feeding of the five
thousand and walking on water. Immediately after these events—on the
next day—Jesus told His disciples:

> I am the bread of life. … No one who comes to Me will ever be
> hungry, and no one who believes in Me will ever be thirsty again.
> **John 6:35**

Because Jesus was working this miracle around Passover, directly after
showing that He was the Messiah, He used an image should have been
powerful in the minds of the disciples. Jesus was the provider of bread,
just as God was the provider of the manna from heaven to the Israelites.

Make a list of things Jesus provides you that magazines
at the checkout counter or infomercials on TV can't.

Honestly, do you believe Jesus is enough? On a scale of 1 to 10, how would you rate your belief that Jesus truly provides everything you need?

1	2	3	4	5	6	7	8	9	10

Not at all   Wholeheartedly

If you believe Jesus will provide what you need, do you still worry that it won't be what you want or that you won't be happy? Explain your answer.

Look at what Paul, the most prolific writer in the New Testament, said about needs, wants, and the source of contentment.

Read Philippians 4:10-14.

I rejoiced in the Lord greatly that once again you renewed your care for me. You were, in fact, concerned about me but lacked the opportunity to show it. I don't say this out of need, for I have learned to be content in whatever circumstances I am. I know both how to have a little, and I know how to have a lot. In any and all circumstances I have learned the secret of being content—whether well fed or hungry, whether in abundance or in need. I am able to do all things through Him who strengthens me. Still, you did well by sharing with me in my hardship.
Philippians 4:10-14

We don't have to look far in our society today to see Paul's famous statement to the church at Philippi: "I am able to do all things through Him who strengthens me" (v. 13). It's sometimes printed on a football player's eye black or displayed in the locker room. People have it tattooed on their arms or their feet.

Unfortunately, we may have lost sight of what Paul was talking about.

Paul began the thought by thanking the church members for their concern for him. He had clearly been through some hard experiences; he had a physical affliction, was constantly in prison for preaching the gospel, and was shipwrecked and beaten on multiple occasions. Perhaps the Philippians believers wrote to him or sent him encouraging gifts when they heard about the latest hardship he was facing.

But as Paul developed the thought, he said something interesting. He said he was able to live on almost nothing, and he knew how to be rich. He knew how to be content in a happy situation or a sad one. He could be at peace with an empty stomach as much as with a full one.

Paul revealed the reason: it was Christ who strengthened him. Verse 13 is less about overcoming whatever adverse situation we find ourselves facing and more about delighting in Christ, no matter where we find ourselves.

A Philippians 4:13 response to losing that football game, then, would be less about knowing you can win because you can do all things through Christ who strengthens you and more about being content with either outcome because you know where your priorities are.

Ask God for wisdom to see your circumstances from His perspective this week and for the ability to focus on being grateful for His sufficiency and grace in every circumstance.

The Path to Life

Week 4

It was Passover, the most important celebration in Jewish culture. This festival looks back to the time of Moses, when God freed the Israelites from their slavery in Egypt. This particular Passover was going to be memorable for an important reason: it would change the entire world.

John 13–19 encompasses one single night and the following day in the life of Jesus and His disciples. It's a tense time in the narrative. The pieces were already in play that would lead to the arrest and crucifixion of the Son of God. As we read, we watch them unfold almost in real time.

As Jesus gathered His closest followers together in an upper room to celebrate the Passover feast, He took the opportunity to make the final preparations they would need before launching out and taking His gospel to the nations.

In John 14 Jesus revealed something about Himself that's essential to His character: He's the only way to get to the Father.

Start

Welcome to session 4 of *Knowing Jesus*. Use the following content to begin your group session together.

In the previous group session you were asked to name some distractions that keep you from seeing God.

> How did acknowledging things that distract you help you resist those distractions?

> How did spending time in the Word this week adjust your focus on Jesus?

> How did Jesus prove His sufficiency for you this week?

> What else was meaningful to you this past week in your reading, journaling, or personal study? Why?

In this session we'll see that Jesus is the exclusive path to the Father—a truth that greatly offends much of the world. In today's video session Robby examines Jesus' claim and explores ways it affects His followers daily.

Pray that God will open your hearts and minds as you watch video session 4.

Watch

Jesus doesn't say, "This is the way." Jesus says, "_____ _____ the way."

The Christian life is a _____.

You Are Important to God

He _____ us in His image.

He _____ us a promise.

He's _____ a place in heaven for us.

He's _____ back to get us.

Discuss

Use the following statements and questions to discuss the video.

When Robby began, he was in a hallway that had one entrance and one exit. The only way to get to the hallway was by the staircase in front of him, and the only way to get to the room behind him was by the hallway.

> **Why do you think it's hard for many people to come to grips with the fact that there's only one way to the Father?**

Read aloud John 14:1-6.

> **What ways do people try to find God other than through Jesus?**

> **How does this passage highlight the need for us to share the gospel?**

> **What excuses are made for being hesitant to share this gospel truth?**

Robby explained the context of Jesus' words in regard to cultural practices in preparation for a wedding. Jewish fathers negotiated a bride price, the son went back to his father's house to build a room for his bride, and then he returned one day to bring his bride home when everything was ready.

> **How does knowing something about Jewish wedding rituals help you understand what Jesus was telling His disciples in these verses?**

While the groom was preparing a place for his bride, there was no sure way to know when he was coming back. It entirely depended on when his father decided the son's room was ready to receive her.

> **Describe what you think was going through the bride's mind while the groom was away.**

Knowing the groom was coming back to get her, the bride needed to make sure she was ready when he arrived. That way when she saw him cresting the hill and coming toward her house, she didn't have to collect her things or prepare herself to be taken away. She was ready at a moment's notice.

> How would you explain what Jesus has gone to do for us?

> What responsibility do we have, like a first-century Jewish bride, once we understand what Jesus has gone to do?

> What does that responsibility look like in the different aspects of your daily life?

Jesus' statement "You know the way to where I am going" (v. 4) may have initially confused the disciples, but it makes perfect sense. The bride wouldn't necessarily know where her new house was, but she certainly knew the way there: the bridegroom was coming back to get her.

In the same way, we can know for certain the only way to get back to the Father. It's through Jesus Christ, the One who's already been there and is coming back for us.

Robby explained that first-century Christians were called the Way because they were so committed to following the Messiah who called Himself by that name.

> If you took stock of your life right now, would you say you're living as if your Groom is coming back to get you?

> How is the knowledge that Jesus is the only way to the Father challenging, encouraging, or insightful for you?

Conclude the group session with the prayer activity on the following page.

Pray

Robby reminded us that the groom's father had to pay a price to secure his son's bride.

> **Read I Corinthians 6:19-20 aloud.**
>
> **Record areas of your life that aren't honoring God for the great price with which He bought you.**
>
> **Keep this list in mind as you go about your daily activities this week. Remember that as we live, we're also preparing ourselves for our Groom, who is coming back to get us.**

You might find yourself meditating on the truth that Jesus is the only way to the Father. One way to be a steward of the period between now and the time when our faith becomes sight is to tell people the good news that God is accessible and that all we have to do to be held in His arms forever is to repent and believe in Jesus Christ.

> **As you share prayer requests and close in prayer, consider the list you made and use it to focus on people around you who need to hear the good news of Jesus Christ.**

Prayer Requests

Encourage members to complete "This Week's Plan" before the next group session.

This Week's Plan

In addition to studying God's Word, work with your group leader to create a plan for personal study, worship, and application between now and the next session. Select from the following optional activities to match your personal preferences and available time.

Worship

[ ] Read your Bible. Complete the reading plan on page 74.

[ ] Spend time with God by engaging with the devotional experience on page 75.

[ ] Connect with God each day through prayer.

Personal Study

[ ] Read and interact with "Lighting the Way" on page 76.

[ ] Read and interact with "The One Who Leads You in Life" on page 80.

Application

[ ] Pray for an opportunity to share the gospel with one person this week.

[ ] Take a 15-minute break in the middle of your day to spend time in prayer. Use this time to extol the majesty of God and to express your gratitude for Jesus' sacrifice that brings us to Him.

[ ] Read the parable of the 10 virgins in Matthew 25:1-13. Consider ways you can keep your wick trimmed.

[ ] Other:

Did you miss the group session?
Video sessions available for purchase at *LifeWay.com/KnowingJesus*

73

Read

Read the following Scripture passages this week. Use the acronym HEAR and the space provided to record your thoughts or action steps.

Day 1: John 10:22-29

Day 2: John 11:1-22

Day 3: John 11:23-44

Day 4: John 11:45-57

Day 5: John 12:1-19

Day 6: John 12:20-36

Day 7: John 12:37-50

Reflect

JESUS AMONG OTHER GODS

"I am the way, the truth, and the life" (John 14:6) is probably the most controversial statement ever made.

As you encounter the Jesus of the Bible, you get to a point at which you draw the conclusion C. S. Lewis did in his book *Mere Christianity:*

> I am trying here to prevent anyone saying the really foolish thing that people often say about Him: "I'm ready to accept Jesus as a great moral teacher, but I don't accept His claim to be God." That is the one thing we must not say. A man who was merely a man and said the sort of things Jesus said would not be a great moral teacher. He would either be a lunatic—on a level with the man who says he is a poached egg—or else he would be the Devil of Hell. You must make your choice. Either this man was, and is, the Son of God: or else a madman or something worse.[1]

This is one of the most spectacular ways Jesus is entirely set apart from the other religious systems and figures of history: His moral teachings are absolutely inseparable from His claim to be God. As we learn more about Jesus, we'll be forced to make a decision, and that decision will probably look like Lewis's trilemma. We'll have to conclude that (1) Jesus was a lunatic, (2) Jesus was a flat-out liar, or (3) Jesus is exactly who He said He was.

Are there areas in your life where you honestly treat what Jesus has said and done as unreasonable to believe or do? Are you living as though you fully believe Jesus was the Son of God?

1. C. S. Lewis, *Mere Christianity,* in *The Complete C. S. Lewis Signature Classics* (New York: HarperOne, 2002), 50–51.

Personal Study 1

LIGHTING THE WAY

The Feast of Booths was one of the most important and dramatic festivals in the Jewish tradition. The Israelites spent a week sleeping in a leafy shelter outside, apart from the comfort of their homes, to recall God's faithfulness to their ancestors as they were wandering through the wilderness on their way to the promised land.

Some of the things the feast included were emblems and ceremonies that represented the pillar of fire that guided the Israelites by night as they traveled (see Ex. 13:21). As the Israelites looked at these symbols and participated in the ceremonies, they would have been struck by the importance of that fire to their ancestors. It's what led them out of their captivity into the promised land. Looking back is one of the most important tools we have for commemorating ways God has worked in our lives.

> **What's your pillar of fire in the wilderness—the thing you can look back on to see ways God has worked in your life?**

When Jesus attended the Feast of Booths in John 7–8, He said something extraordinary:

> I am the light of the world. Anyone who follows Me will never walk in the darkness but will have the light of life.
> **John 8:12**

In the context of this feast, Jesus was revealing that He's the One who saves and leads His people. We have to follow Him, walking in the light, since He's the only way to way to God the Father (see John 14:6).

What the Light Does

Read these passages about light and identify the purpose you think the light serves in each of them.

Psalm 27:1

Isaiah 9:1-2

Isaiah 49:6

Ephesians 5:8-14

As we see, light serves multiple purposes in Scripture. It's paralleled with salvation in Psalm 27, it represents the end of oppressive gloom in Isaiah 9, it's God's message to the nations in Isaiah 49, and it drives away darkness in Ephesians 5. These are only a few examples of what Scripture says light does.

Which one of the previous verses resonates most personally with you? Why does it resonate with you right now?

Who the Light Is

Even when we're at our darkest, God proved that He isn't in the business of leaving us on our own. Even though it may be dark at times, He's our ever-present hope and salvation.

When Jesus was talking to the Israelites in John 8:12, they were at the Feast of Booths. That's why He brought up light in the first place. They may have even been standing near one of the reminders of the pillar of fire that guided the ancient Israelites through the desert at night.

Think about that connection. As the people reminisced about God's guidance during a dark time in their history, Jesus said He's the light of the entire world. He was saying, "This light was helpful back then, and it may even help you remember God's faithfulness. You can also recall a hundred other things from Scripture that light does. I'm all those and more. Everything light is and has been, I AM."

> Think back to the different purposes of light you identified in Scripture and the one that resonates most personally with you. How has Jesus proved Himself to be the Light in your life?

> What area of your life most desperately needs light to shine on it?

Where the Light Is Found

Look again at Jesus' statement in John 8:12:

> I am the light of the world. Anyone who follows Me will
> never walk in the darkness but will have the light of life.
> **John 8:12**

Not only does Jesus tell us who He is, but He also tells us how to get Him. We only have to follow Him. We see that call throughout the Gospels, when He called fishermen and tax collectors to "Follow Me" (Matt. 4:19; Mark 1:17; Luke 5:27; John 1:43). He said it to Peter at the end of the Book of John: "What is that to you? As for you, follow Me" (John 21:22). And He still says it to us today.

If we want to live in the light and find our way to the Father, we have one option: follow the One who is the light.

Psalm 119:105 tells us:

> Your word is a lamp for my feet
> and a light on my path.
> **Psalm 119:105**

What's the next step you need to take to better follow Jesus, the Word of God made flesh, the Light of the world?

Personal Study 2

THE ONE WHO LEADS YOU IN LIFE

Most Western Christians have little idea what first-century Israeli shepherds were like. This gap in our understanding makes passages like the following seem just out of reach, as if a tiny piece of information is missing. Jesus told those gathered around Him in John 10:

> I assure you: Anyone who doesn't enter the sheep pen by the door but climbs in some other way, is a thief and a robber. The one who enters by the door is the shepherd of the sheep. The doorkeeper opens it for him, and the sheep hear his voice. He calls his own sheep by name and leads them out.
> **John 10:1-3**

Ancient shepherds in Israel often corralled their sheep into a pen for the night. This practice served two purposes: to make sure none of the sheep wandered off and to make sure no predators came in to snatch them. Once the shepherd got the sheep inside, he did something remarkable. He lay down in the doorway of the pen. The shepherd literally became the door of the sheep pen.

Why do you think Jesus used the metaphor of a shepherd to teach the first-century Israelites about Himself?

If Jesus were speaking to a crowd today, what metaphors do you think He would use?

Calling the Sheep

Larger pens were maintained on the outskirts of the city. Here any shepherd coming to the city could leave his sheep, which would go and mingle with the other shepherds' flocks. When that shepherd returned, he called to his sheep, and they came to the gate, ready to leave. The rest of the sheep would stay where they were since their shepherds hadn't called them.

Jesus continued:

> When he has brought all his own outside, he goes ahead of
> them. The sheep follow him because they recognize his voice.
> They will never follow a stranger; instead they will run away
> from him, because they don't recognize the voice of strangers.
> **John 10:4-5**

How do you recognize your Shepherd's voice?

What "strangers" call to you, wanting you to follow them instead?

Keeping the Sheep Safe

When the sheep settled down and the shepherd slept across the doorway, the sheep knew he wasn't going to let anything into the pen that might hurt them. They also knew he wasn't going to let sheep in that didn't belong to his flock. If he did, those sheep wouldn't know whom to follow when the shepherd called for them.

Jesus drew on this understanding when he continued:

> I assure you: I am the door of the sheep. All who came before Me are
> thieves and robbers, but the sheep didn't listen to them. I am the door.
> If anyone enters by Me, he will be saved and will come in and go out
> and find pasture. A thief comes only to steal and to kill and to destroy.
> I have come so that they may have life and to have it in abundance.
> **John 10:7-10**

When the sheep find their safety behind the true Door, they know they'll
be safe, but Jesus adds further blessings. His sheep can go in and out and
find pasture. What wonderful freedom we have in Jesus, who's the Door
to the kingdom of God! Jesus, as the Door, is the picture of a good leader
rather than a tyrant, who would keep every head of sheep near at all times
and would restrict all their movement. Jesus brings liberty, not bondage.
His yoke is easy, and His burden is light (see Matt. 11:30).

What have you done to enter the flock of Christ?

What freedom does Jesus grant you as His sheep?

What security does Jesus provide you?

Leading the Sheep

In Jesus' day a shepherd let his sheep find pasture in order to get their nourishment. The sheep followed him around until he brought them to a place with plenty of grass to eat. The shepherd provided for all their needs.

As sheep in our Shepherd's flock, we're called to follow our Shepherd only. He isn't like any other Shepherd before or since He came, so He doesn't operate the same way any of the others do.

> **What will change about the way you live your everyday life when you decide to turn and follow Jesus completely?**

> **What's the most difficult part of following Jesus for you?**

Jesus didn't tell us that following Him would be carefree. In fact, He called His way the narrow one, meaning it's frequently more difficult (see Matt. 7:13-14). But what we receive from the Good Shepherd, the Bread of Life, is something infinitely more rewarding than anything the world could offer us. Whatever the world shows us is subject to change and decay, and most of it is specifically designed to fulfill you only as long as it takes to introduce the next version of it. Jesus' promise is eternal and unchanging: "Follow Me, and I will always be more than enough for you."

> **Close your time in prayer, asking for strength to continue walking after the only One who will feed you with everything you need, no matter how attractive other options seem.**

Experiencing the Kingdom

Week 5

The sheer concept of God—the everlasting Creator of the entire universe who's bigger than the stars He made, more powerful than the storms He controls, and seated on His throne in a realm of splendor we can't even imagine—is difficult for some people to come to terms with.

We all have a tendency to think that way. If we aren't careful, we can slip into the same trap of thinking that what we see is all there is. Or we may begin to place eternal significance on things that are going to go away.

Through a conversation with a Pharisee named Nicodemus, we'll see how Jesus shed some light on a subject that escaped even one of the most renowned teachers of Israel: the kingdom of God. We'll also see how understanding what Jesus told Nicodemus changed the course of his life.

Start

In the previous group session you considered the great price that was paid and the preparation God made for a loving covenant relationship with you.

> **How did understanding the tremendous value your Heavenly Father sees in you affect the way you saw your life this past week?**

> **When was it helpful this week to remember that your life is a walk of faith? Were there times when you felt discouraged that you weren't further along? Were you encouraged to know that you needed to take each moment step-by-step?**

> **In what ways did the exclusive nature of knowing God by following the Son affect your daily walk?**

> **What else was meaningful to you this past week in your reading, journaling, or personal study? Why?**

In this session we'll see where Nicodemus went when he had questions. We're going to look at his conversation with Jesus and come to realize that nothing has changed in the two thousand years since this conversation occurred. The kingdom of God is at hand, and we're each responsible for where we place our faith.

Pray that God will open your hearts and minds as you watch video session 5.

Watch

The kingdom of God was not _____. It was
_____incarnational_____.

The Hebrews knew that the kingdom of God was not just a Person in Jesus,
but it was a _____power_____ and a _____presense_____.

The kingdom of God is not a _____ place you have to wait
to go to. It's a present power in your life _____.

When God is _____ and _____ in our life,
when God is calling the shots, that's how the kingdom comes today.

If a person is born once, they die _____twice_____. But if you're born
twice, you only die _____once_____.

While Jesus' death is sufficient for all, it's only effectual for those who
_____ and _____.

Discuss

Use the following statements and questions to discuss the video.

Robby mentioned that Nicodemus's coming to Jesus at night was significant in at least three ways:

1. Rabbis generally studied and learned at night.

2. The cloak of darkness would have made him less likely to be discovered by someone.

3. Night and darkness are frequently used to describe a heart that's far from God.

Read John 3:1-18.

What do you typically do to get answers to spiritual questions? What books or study tools have been helpful? To whom do you go with questions?

In what ways has this group been a safe place to ask honest questions?

When was a time you had an honest question but were afraid to ask it in case someone overheard you? What was/is the question?

Robby mentioned several ways God is a coming-down God and explained that other people before Christ had prophesied the coming of the kingdom of God.

How does it change your perspective to know that God has initiated a relationship with you?

Although we don't know Nicodemus's immediate reaction, Robby pointed out that this isn't the last time we see him in Scripture. At the end of Jesus' life, Nicodemus made provisions for Jesus after He died on the cross. His actions seem to prove his loyalty to and belief in Jesus Christ as the Son of God.

> **If someone were writing your biography and wanted to include something that demonstrated your belief in Jesus, what do you think they would write?**

> **As a Christian, how do you want to be remembered?**

Robby concluded by asking whether you have been born again, experiencing the kingdom of God in your own life. It's important to take time and encourage one another as believers by sharing our stories.

> **What did you first know about Jesus?**

> **How would you describe the lostness or darkness in your life before believing in Jesus?**

> **When were you born again?**

> **How has the new birth changed your life for the sake of God's kingdom?**

> **Although we most often stop with John 3:16, why is it important to recognize the urgency and seriousness of verses 17-18?**

Conclude the group session with the prayer activity on the following page.

Pray

Read aloud the words of Jesus in John 3:19-21.

Take three minutes to reflect on your life, thoughts, and desires. Are there things you would rather shove into a cupboard than expose? List them. You don't have to show your list to anybody, but simply writing it down is important.

Take three minutes to pray for the strength to release those things, whether they're sins, strongholds, guilt, or fear. Lay them at the feet of Jesus, who was raised up so that we could live. Finally, pray that the Lord will give you someone to whom you can confess the things in your life you would like to hide.

Prayer Requests

Encourage members to complete "This Week's Plan" before the next group session.

This Week's Plan

In addition to studying God's Word, work with your group leader to create a plan for personal study, worship, and application between now and the next session. Select from the following optional activities to match your personal preferences and available time.

Worship

[ ] Read your Bible. Complete the reading plan on page 92.

[ ] Spend time with God by engaging with the devotional experience on page 93.

[ ] Connect with God each day through prayer.

Personal Study

[ ] Read and interact with "Sin: Our Problem" on page 94.

[ ] Read and interact with "The Sinner" on page 98.

Application

[ ] Take a walk in a public place and watch the people around you. Ask yourself, *What do these people want most?* As different things come to mind, consider ways Jesus can fulfill those desires.

[ ] Spend a morning expanding the list you made in your prayer activity. Take time to present each item to God.

[ ] Read Numbers 21:4-9. Record ways that passage helps you understand Jesus' words to Nicodemus in John 3:14-15.

[ ] Other:

Did you miss the group session?
Video sessions available for purchase at *LifeWay.com/KnowingJesus*

91

Read

Read the following Scripture passages this week. Use the acronym HEAR and the space provided to record your thoughts or action steps.

Day 1: John 13:1-17

Day 2: John 13:18-38

Day 3: John 14:1-14

Day 4: John 14:15-31

Day 5: John 15:1-17

Day 6: John 15:18-27

Day 7: John 16

Reflect

CAMELS AND THE KINGDOM OF GOD

Deciding that earthly riches were better than following Jesus, a rich young man walked away from Him. Jesus turned and addressed His disciples:

> I assure you: It will be hard for a rich person to enter the kingdom of heaven! Again I tell you, it is easier for a camel to go through the eye of a needle than for a rich person to enter the kingdom of God.
> **Matthew 19:23-24**

For years pastors have taught that this passage referred to a literal gate in Jerusalem where a camel would have to stoop down without any baggage and crawl on its knees in order to pass through. It makes for a nice sermon illustration, but there's a problem: no such gate existed. What Jesus meant is what He said: it would be easier for the biggest animal in Jerusalem to pass through the smallest tool available than it would be for someone in love with his money to follow Jesus.

The phrase *kingdom of heaven* is used 31 times in the Book of Matthew alone. Contrary to popular belief, it isn't just a reference to a future dwelling place; rather, it's a present reality!

When Jesus referred to the kingdom of heaven, He meant something we can experience today. Paul described that experience like this: "Our citizenship is in heaven, from which we also eagerly wait for a Savior, the Lord Jesus Christ" (Phil. 3:20). Being a citizen of the kingdom of heaven means we aren't concerned with earthly riches but rather with bringing glory to Him who created us, saved us, and set us free: Jesus Christ.

> **What's the one thing you would have trouble letting go of if Jesus asked you to drop it in order to follow Him? What do you need to lay down in order to put the kingdom of God first?**

Personal Study 1

SIN: OUR PROBLEM

When Jesus spoke to Nicodemus in John 3, He directly referred to an influential event in Israel's history, described in Numbers 21:4-9.

> They set out from Mount Hor by way of the Red Sea to bypass the land of Edom, but the people became impatient because of the journey. The people spoke against God and Moses: "Why have you led us up from Egypt to die in the wilderness? There is no bread or water, and we detest this wretched food!" Then the LORD sent poisonous snakes among the people, and they bit them so that many Israelites died.
> **Numbers 21:4-6**

The Israelites repeated a similar pattern of rebellion throughout their history in the first five books of the Bible. It looked like this: the Israelites rebelled, God revealed their sin, and they repented and turned back to Him.

Have you ever been in a cycle of rebellion like the one the Israelites were stuck in? Explain what happened.

Why is it easy for us to get stuck in this cycle as the Israelites did?

In this passage what caused the Israelites' cycle of rebellion to start over again? What's your equivalent of their grumbling and complaining?

The Israelites' complaints were demonstrations of active rebellion against God's provision and generosity. We call acts of rebellion against God, even if they're just attitudes of the heart, sin. When it comes down to it, we sin every time we place anything in a position of greater importance than God.

But as we'll see, God provided an escape from their cycle of rebellion.

Moses: Israel's Intercessor

> The people then came to Moses and said, "We have sinned by speaking against the LORD and against you. Intercede with the LORD so that He will take the snakes away from us." And Moses interceded for the people.
> **Numbers 21:7**

An intercessor is someone who makes an appeal to an authority figure on behalf of someone else.

Why do you think the Israelites wanted someone to appeal to God on their behalf?

Have you ever asked someone to make an appeal on your behalf, perhaps because you felt shame, inadequacy, or a sense that you were in over your head? Describe what happened and how you felt.

The Israelites recognized that they had been wrong and wanted to take steps toward fixing the relationships they had broken by their sin, but they didn't know how to ask, and they didn't know what was required of them. They needed someone to take the burden of guilt off their shoulders for them.

How do you think the Israelites felt, knowing Moses was going to speak to God on their behalf?

Salvation: God's Solution

The LORD said to Moses, "Make a snake image and mount it on a pole. When anyone who is bitten looks at it, he will recover." So Moses made a bronze snake and mounted it on a pole. Whenever someone was bitten, and he looked at the bronze snake, he recovered.
Numbers 21:8-9

The Israelites weren't saved by faith in an image but by faith in God's provision to cover the punishment for their sins.

How has God removed the penalty of sin from your shoulders? What should that lifted weight drive you to do?

What's the ultimate end of a life lived in sin?

How did God provide a way out for the Israelites in Numbers 21?

What could they have done on their own to save themselves?

What's the only thing God required of the Israelites to be saved from the certain death that waited for them?

Although the idea of snakes and poles may seem unusual to you, it was not only a means of salvation in the moment but also a foreshadowing of God's work to ultimately save people from sin and death. It's still a matter of life and death as to whether you and the people around you will cry out to God and look in faith toward His provision of an intercessor.

Jesus used this powerful image to emphasize the role of faith in salvation:

> Just as Moses lifted up the snake in the wilderness, so the Son of Man must be lifted up, so that everyone who believes in Him will have eternal life. For God loved the world in this way: He gave His One and Only Son, so that everyone who believes in Him will not perish but have eternal life.
> **John 3:14-16**

How does understanding the context make John 3:16, arguably the most famous verse in the Bible, come alive for you?

Because of Jesus' perfect sacrifice, we're entirely free from the guilt of our sin. We've received life by grace alone, not by anything we've earned for ourselves.

Close your study time in prayer, thanking God for showing mercy to people who don't deserve it and for giving life to people who deserve death. Praise Jesus as the source of your salvation.

Personal Study 2

THE SINNER

What does *worship* mean? For many, worship is the second half of *praise*, as in *praise and worship*. It's the 25 minutes before a sermon on Sunday morning. It's perhaps even the act of giving an offering.

What does *worship* actually mean?

Record the definition of *worship* that pops into your head.

You've already studied Nicodemus; now you're going to read about another person who shares qualities we all feel describe us at times. She was the polar opposite of Nicodemus in every way, but they shared the most important thing in common: they needed Jesus to help them understand the truth about God and about how to live in relationship with Him.

Read John 4:4-26.

Put yourself in this woman's shoes for the rest of this personal study. Try to see this encounter with Jesus through her eyes. It's common for you to be at the well at this hour (around noon, when the hot Middle Eastern sun is highest in the sky) by yourself. Most women have already been to the well to fetch the day's water and are now at home taking care of housework or tending to the children.

Yet here you are, probably because nobody else is around. You carry a deep sense of shame with you.

Have you ever intentionally avoided other company—either because you were embarrassed, grieving, shameful, angry, or another reason? What kinds of emotions would you feel if someone, particularly a religious teacher, approached you during this time?

Suddenly a man who's clearly a rabbi sits next to you as you struggle with your heavy water pot. He asks for water. You don't mind giving Him some, but you're curious and a little bit skeptical about why He's talking to you in the first place.

Your people and His people have a history of intense hatred for each other. So it's doubly strange that a member of the religious establishment is giving you the time of day, much less asking you for a favor.

You ask Him about it, and He gives you an answer you weren't expecting:

> If you knew the gift of God, and who is saying to you, "Give Me a drink," you would ask Him, and He would give you living water.
> **John 4:10**

Record some things you ask God for.

Try to evaluate your list from God's perspective. Are the things you want the things God wants, or are they different?

You're confused again. The well you're drawing water from is old and famous. It's the well established by Jacob thousands of years before. You assume the stranger already knows this, given that He's a rabbi, but it's worth mentioning again. You're fine with your relationship with God. You've done things this way for years and years.

But the rabbi hits another chord in your heart with the words He says next:

> Everyone who drinks from this water will get thirsty again.
> But whoever drinks from the water that I will give him will never
> get thirsty again—ever! In fact, the water I will give him will
> become a well of water springing up within him for eternal life.
> **John 4:13-14**

How do you form your ideas about God? For example, does someone tell you, do you seek them for yourself, or do you rely on the beliefs you've always had?

There's something strange about this man. You look for the easy way out and just ask Him for this water. It may save you some trips to the well in the middle of the day. You won't have to come out anymore and risk running into someone who'll confront you about the things you're trying to hide from them.

But then something horrible happens. He asks you a question pointed straight at the thing you've been avoiding. You try dodging it, but He's relentless. It's as though He can see past every thick door and padlock you've set up to keep that secret buried. It's as if He understands why you've come to the well at so late an hour.

You didn't bring up this topic, but the man has somehow brought it into the open anyway. You feel exposed, naked. You try changing the subject to get away from this horrible feeling in your chest, but He brings down the final hammer. After He's exposed the innermost things about you so that you have nothing else to hide, He explains how you're supposed to worship.

"True worshipers will worship the Father in spirit and truth" (John 4:23), He says. You understand it completely now. The longer you hold pieces of yourself back from God's use, the more they'll fester and grow into something dangerous and poisonous. Worshiping the Father means letting go—of yourself, your desires, your preconceived notions, your sin— and asking Him to use every bit of it for His glory.

> **How does it make you feel to know that Jesus is fully aware of your past, present, and future?**

> **What are things you've held back from God?**

> **How can God use these things to bring glory to Himself?**

> **Pray now that God's work through Jesus Christ, the Living Water, will transform every part of your life into an act of worship.**

Seeking in Our Doubt

Aside from Jesus' inner circle of disciples (Peter, James, and John), Thomas is perhaps the most famous. He didn't write a Gospel, He didn't speak a great number of lines in Scripture, and his post-Gospel history is largely speculative. Yet we remember him vividly.

He's the doubter. Doubting Thomas, we call him.

In just a few lines his reputation has been sealed in our minds—though perhaps unfairly.

God is more remarkable the more we see Him and the more we see those He uses. He specifically chose Thomas because he represented what Jesus was most interested in. Therefore, Thomas is someone we can learn from.

Thomas may not be the doubter after all. Maybe it's time to think of him as something different. This week we're going to explore what true seekers of Christ look like.

Start

Welcome to session 6 of *Knowing Jesus*. Use the following content to begin your group session together.

In the previous group session you were asked to consider secrets you were keeping hidden deep in your heart.

Did you do anything this week to expose those things to God?

Did you seek out anybody to share your burdens with? Explain how that felt.

What else was meaningful to you this past week in your reading, journaling, or personal study? Why?

In this session we'll meet a disciple of Jesus who was prone to internalizing things, who was probably highly introverted, who has received an unfair reputation over the years, and yet who was perhaps one of Jesus' most honest seekers and most devoted followers. Let's watch as Robby explains who Thomas was so that we can try to be more like him.

Pray that God will open your hearts and minds as you watch the video for session 6.

Watch

Why Thomas Was a Seeker, Not a Doubter

Thomas was _____ to Jesus.

Thomas desired to _____ about Jesus.

Thomas's doubt leads to _____.

Thomas is not an unbelieving _____. He's a distressed
_____.

Thomas is longing for one final encounter with his rabbi,
_____.

God can use our _____ to deepen our faith.

It's not how you _____. It's how you _____.

Discuss

Use the following statements and questions to discuss the video.

What preconceived ideas about Thomas did you have before hearing Robby's teaching?

Did Robby's teaching change your opinion of Thomas? Why or why not?

Robby explored three different Scripture passages that mention Thomas.

Read aloud John 11:11-16.

As Jesus informed His disciples that they were going back to Bethany, where He had just been rejected for claiming to be one with the Father, His disciples knew precisely the kind of danger He was in. They first tried to talk Him out of going by insisting that Lazarus would get better.

When have you been hesitant to trust God? What kinds of excuses do you often offer for not doing what the Lord calls you to do?

Notice what Thomas said in verse 16: "Let's go so that we may die with Him."

Is there anything you would be willing to die for? If so, what?

Read aloud John 14:1-7.

Thomas's question proves the second aspect of his nature: he was devoted not only to Jesus but also to the truth. He wanted to understand even if it meant asking something Jesus may have considered a dumb question.

How committed are you to the truth, even if it's difficult to hear?

Read aloud John 20:24-29.

Thomas was noticeably absent when Jesus appeared the first time. Robby speculated that the reason Thomas was missing wasn't that he feared for his life (he had already proved that he was willing to die for Jesus) but that he was so wracked with sadness and grief that he couldn't bear to be around others so soon after his Master died.

> If you had been in Thomas's position, how would you have reacted to the news that Jesus was back?

> What kind of proof do you ask from Jesus to prove Himself?

When Jesus finally appeared to Thomas, He presented him with exactly the evidence he had asked to see. Jesus knew the heart of His disciple and was prepared to remove every barrier to his belief.

> What proves to you that Jesus is who He says He is?

> Would you consider yourself a passive believer or an active seeker of Jesus?

> What about this account quells a fear or doubt you have about who Jesus is?

> What has been challenging, encouraging, or insightful from the case of the famous doubter Thomas?

Conclude the group session with the prayer activity on the following page.

Pray

If there's anything Thomas teaches us, it's that it's OK to ask questions. We see questions throughout Scripture. We see people pressing forward in their faith in spite of doubt, and that's OK because the opposite of belief isn't doubt but disobedience. Thomas may have had his doubts, but they weren't doubts leading to skepticism; they were doubts leading to his proclamation that Jesus was both Lord and God (see John 4:28).

Make a list of doubts you have about God.

Spend a few minutes in prayer bringing each one of your doubts to Jesus. Thank Him for being true even when you can't see tangible evidence. Acknowledge that although you don't have all the answers, you'll follow Him in faith anyway.

Prayer Requests

Decide what you will study next as a group. Encourage members to complete "This Week's Plan" before the next time you meet.

This Week's Plan

In addition to studying God's Word, work with your group leader to create a plan for personal study, worship, and application between now and the next session. Select from the following optional activities to match your personal preferences and available time.

Worship

[ ] Read your Bible. Complete the reading plan on page 110.

[ ] Spend time with God by engaging with the devotional experience on page 111.

[ ] Connect with God each day through prayer.

Personal Study

[ ] Read and interact with "The Speaker Among the Dunes" on page 112.

[ ] Read and interact with "The Seeker Under the Tree" on page 116.

Application

[ ] Reflect on the things you've learned about Jesus through this study of John's Gospel. What questions have been answered? How have you seen Jesus more clearly? What's that fresh sight leading you to do?

[ ] Read Job 38–39 in light of any doubts you have. How does God address those doubts? How can a new perspective on who God is help alleviate your doubts?

[ ] Take a friend who's struggling with belief out for coffee. Take time to listen to them. Encourage them even if you don't have all the answers.

[ ] Other:

Did you miss the group session?
Video sessions available for purchase at *LifeWay.com/KnowingJesus*

109

Read

Read the following Scripture passages this week. Use the acronym HEAR and the space provided to record your thoughts or action steps.

Day 1: John 17

Day 2: John 18:1-14

Day 3: John 18:15-40

Day 4: John 19:1-27

Day 5: John 19:28-42

Day 6: John 20

Day 7: John 21

Reflect

AS FOR YOU

Among the last lines of John's Gospel are the final portion of Peter's recon-
ciliation with Jesus.

Read John 21:20-22.

In our Christian walk it's inevitable that we'll have questions along the way.

We'll say, "The world is full of terror and uncertainty." He will say,
as He did to Peter: "What is that to you?"

"I have so many questions, and the answers never seem to come. Every time
I ask, You seem silent. No matter what I find myself doing, the further
I look down the road, the more meaningless it becomes, and the more
unfulfilled I am."

"What is that to you?"

"As for you," He says to the searcher, to the griever, to the widow,
to the orphan.

"As for you," He says to the sick and the healthy, to the rich and the poor,
to the invalid and the introvert and the irate.

"As for you," you who are searching, you who are questioning, you who are
eating, drinking, and being merry to forget that tomorrow you'll die, who
follow forest paths we're told will lead us to where we think we want to be.

"As for you, follow Me."

Personal Study 1

THE SPEAKER AMONG THE DUNES

When it comes to the truth about Jesus, it should stir something deep in our hearts and minds until it overflows in worship. On seeing the resurrected Lord, a so-called doubting disciple made one of the boldest declarations in all the New Testament:

> Thomas responded to Him, "My Lord and my God!"
> **John 20:28**

Those are powerful words! There's no question as to whether Thomas remained with the deepest question of his heart unanswered.

Jesus met Thomas where he was, revealing the truth in a way Thomas could understand. The disciples experienced the truth of Jesus so that the message of the gospel could spread throughout the world and throughout history. The fact that you're reading this Bible study right now—and, hopefully, believe in Jesus as your Lord and your God—is evidence that eyewitnesses like Thomas proclaimed the good news of the resurrection.

Remember Jesus' response to Thomas?

> Because you have seen Me, you have believed.
> Those who believe without seeing are blessed.
> **John 20:29**

The gospel didn't begin after Jesus' resurrection. As we've seen throughout this study, God had promised to send a Savior and King. Immediately before Jesus called His disciples to begin His three-year ministry, a man named John called people to prepare for the kingdom of God.

John the Baptist is known as one of the most eccentric characters in Scripture. With an unusual style of dress and an interesting diet, he was thoroughly devoted to preparing people's hearts for the coming Messiah.

When people took notice of this strange man and heard the content of his preaching, they asked whether he was the Messiah they were looking for. He replied simply and profoundly:

> I am a voice of one crying out in the wilderness:
> Make straight the way of the Lord.
> **John 1:23**

John's words proved a number of things:

1. He knew Scripture well.

2. He understood his purpose.

3. He was entirely devoted to Jesus, the coming Messiah.

Let's read about and explore John's testimony of who Jesus was.

Read John 1:26-34.

The first thing we see about John is his humility. He had lived the life of a prophet, wearing a coat of hair and a leather belt, prophesying to people who probably had mixed feelings about him.

John then said he wasn't even worthy to untie the sandals of the One who was to come after Him, speaking of the Messiah.

When you approach Jesus, what's your attitude toward Him?

What can you do to prepare yourself to meet Jesus?

What can you do to prepare others to meet Jesus?

As John preached, he also baptized people who repented of their sin and believed in the coming Messiah. The idea of repentance and belief in Jesus is older than His ministry—and older than His death on the cross. The truth that atonement for sin requires the blood of a sacrifice began in the garden of Eden. An animal had to die to cover the nakedness Adam and Eve uncovered through their sin. The same idea was built into the grueling sacrificial system the ancient Israelites practiced for thousands of years.

What phrase did John use for Jesus that directly linked Him to the sacrifice that covers sin?

What image is suggested by John's description of Jesus as "the Lamb of God" (John 1:29), especially in regard to the Jewish sacrificial system?

How does recognizing Jesus as the Lamb of God affect the way you live?

Even before Jesus' identity as the Messiah was revealed, John was doing everything he could to ensure that others would recognize Him. Though we live in a time when the Messiah has already come, John's testimony is a poignant reminder that we can still act as beacons pointing to the Savior.

In what ways is your life a walking testament to the risen Messiah?

What can you do among the people you're around to point them to Jesus?

If someone were recording your actions in a book, in what ways would they say you live as John did by helping people prepare their hearts to encounter Christ?

What do you consider to be your purpose on earth?

How can you live out this purpose in a way that honors God?

Close your study time in prayer, thanking God for revealing Jesus to you. Ask for boldness to declare Jesus as the Son of God, who takes away the sin of the world.

Personal Study 2

THE SEEKER UNDER THE TREE

Nathanael isn't one of the disciples we would likely pick if told to select one at random. Frankly, not a lot is written about him in the Bible. Nonetheless, the account of the way Jesus selected him to be His follower is a remarkable one that deserves our full attention.

Before looking at this account, let's take an inventory to determine how we would have responded if we had been in Nathanael's shoes.

If Jesus came up to you while you were going about a normal day, what do you think you would be doing?

Imagine that Jesus hadn't come yet. What do you think you would be looking for in the Messiah when He finally showed up?

Can you think of an area near you or a group you're aware of that you think is full of people who are, for lack of a better term, nuts?

Read John 1:43-51.

We immediately see that Philip responded with urgency to Jesus' call to follow Him. His first action was to go find Nathanael. When he found Nathanael, Philip said something interesting: "We've found Him!"

Based on this exclamation, what do you think Philip
and Nathanael's conversations usually consisted of?

How would you describe your conversations with the people
to whom you're closest?

How important is it to you to keep the things of God
on the forefront of your mind?

Philip told Nathanael they had found the Messiah and that His name was
Jesus of Nazareth. Nathanael's response, "Can anything good come out of
Nazareth?" (v. 46), might have sounded like a strange question, but it was
a legitimate one. The people in Nazareth were known for being fanatical
about the Messiah, to the point that they were probably pointing to possible
candidates in every promising prospect who came along.

What preconceived notions do you think people who haven't
personally encountered Jesus have about Him?

Philip didn't respond to Nathanael's prejudicial comment with an argument
but with the far more convincing "Come and see for yourself."

As you talk to people about Jesus, which do you try to do more: convince them with persuasive arguments about who He is or lead them to a place where they can discover Jesus for themselves? Why?

How do you think you could prepare someone's heart for an encounter with Jesus?

Jesus' words that convinced Nathanael were simple: "I saw you under the fig tree" (v. 50). "Under the fig tree" may not hold much meaning for us today, but in first-century Israel rabbis used this phrase to describe meditating on Scripture.

Think of the implications. Jesus knew Nathanael first, and He knew him as he was studying Scripture. The Word made flesh is always discovered first and foremost in His Word.

Look at Nathanael's response:

> "Rabbi," Nathanael replied, "You are the
> Son of God! You are the King of Israel!"
> **John 1:49**

Would Jesus be able to say He found you while you were studying His Word?

How committed are you to searching out the One who's the Word in His Word?

Just as Nathanael met Jesus under the fig tree, I hope Jesus has revealed Himself to you through your study of Scripture during the past six weeks. As this study of the Gospel of John comes to a close, remember these three things, if nothing else:

1. Jesus is who He says He is.

2. Jesus is still alive and active today.

3. Jesus is always found in His Word.

John wrote his Gospel for the express purpose of giving you the proof you need to know Jesus is the Son of God:

> These are written so that you may believe Jesus is the Messiah,
> the Son of God, and by believing you may have life in His name.
> **John 20:31**

Armed with this knowledge, you're faced with a simple but life-altering question: What will you do with it?

Pray that as you live by Jesus' name, you'll continue to grow as His disciple. Pray that the more you know Him, they more you'll love Him; the more you love Him, the more you'll obey Him; and the more you obey Him, the more He will manifest Himself to you.

Leader Guide

Opening and Closing Group Sessions

Always try to engage each person at the beginning of a group session. Once a person speaks, even if only to answer a generic question, he or she is more likely to speak up later about more personal matters.

You may want to begin each session by reviewing the previous week's personal study. This review provides context for the new session and opportunities to share relevant experiences, application, or truths learned between sessions. Then set up the theme of the study to prepare personal expectations.

Always open and close the session with prayer, recognizing that only the Holy Spirit provides understanding and transformation in our lives. (The prayer suggestions provided in each session help focus members on Scripture, key truths, and personal application from the week's teaching.)

Remember that your goal isn't just meaningful discussion but discipleship.

Session 1: Revealing His Identity

It's important to engage people immediately. Simple questions not only get people talking but also help people get to know one another. This sets an easy precedent for opening up about our personal lives.

The opening questions about daily activity and rest introduce the context of this session. In the midst of busyness, Jesus revealed His identity.

How does this cyclical process help you understand discipleship?

This question establishes discipleship and growth as an ongoing process.

Read Mark 6:47-50 and John 6:16-20.

Always keep God's Word central in your time together. This prevents people from getting off track and veering into speculation or opinion. Even though Robby is teaching on the video, the goal is for people to walk away knowing what the Bible says, not just what a pastor or a group leader says. Asking group members to read aloud also invites greater participation and encourages confidence as they "lead" in that moment.

In John's account what physical details in each verse help set the emotional tone? (This also applies to other study questions.)

Asking questions about details in the Scripture passage is more than an exercise in reading comprehension. They help group members focus on and process what they're reading, drawing them into the scene.

The details included in each account provide a sense of being overwhelmed.

What was something significant Robby pointed out in Mark 6:48?

The detail Mark included—that Jesus meant to pass them by—wasn't an afterthought by the author. In the Jewish mind it would have been an explicit link to the account of Moses in Exodus 33:22. Take some time to discuss how Jesus (as an Eastern rabbi) revealed His identity and the importance of understanding biblical context.

If you've reached the same conclusion the disciples did in Matthew 14:33, what convinced you? (This applies to any application question.)

Always help people identify personal implications of the study. Prayer based on the Scripture text and application of the truth are key to spiritual growth.

Session 2: The Power of Faith

Start by reviewing the previous group session and asking group members to share any insights or experiences related to the previous week's study. This step is important, so allow enough time to share and review, but be careful to protect the time needed to watch and discuss this week's video.

How is Robby's definition of *faith* encouraging, helpful, or convicting?

It's helpful to transition from the video teaching to group discussion with a question that's broad enough to allow everyone to respond to the teaching but also specific enough to guide responses. (This also helps you assess the needs of your group.)

In what ways was the royal official in Cana a stark contrast to the people in Jesus' hometown?

The people in Jesus' hometown were probably so familiar with Him that they couldn't move past Jesus, the man, whom they had known for 30 years. We know, of course, that they weren't really familiar with Him, for if they had been, they would have known who He was.

This is also a warning to us to avoid a false familiarity with Jesus or to think we already know everything about Him.

We know the official had faith because he (I) traveled a great distance, knowing if he could find Jesus, his daughter would be healed, and (2) departed for home without insisting that Jesus come with him—that at Jesus' word alone the girl would be healed.

Robby said the opposite of faith isn't unbelief but disobedience.

Was that surprising? Explain your reaction to that statement.

James 2:14,18 says, "What good is it, my brothers, if someone says he has faith but does not have works? Can his faith save him? But someone will say, 'You have faith, and I have works.' Show me your faith without works, and I will show you faith from my works."

Point back to the example of the royal official's faithful obedience. Use the previous and following verses from James to be sure group members internalize the reality that belief of a fact doesn't become faith until action is taken. In fact, knowing God's Word but not obeying it is worthless. It's sin.

James 4:17 says, "It is a sin for the person who knows to do what is good and doesn't do it."

How has God used suffering in your life to strengthen your faith?

These questions will bring the faith talk close to home by encouraging introspection and personal accounts. Again, this is a great way for you as the leader to encourage transparency by being transparent yourself.

On a scale of 1 to 10, 1 being dead and 10 being vibrant, how would you rate your faith? Explain your answer.

Questions using a scale of 1 to 10 or multiple-choice questions may feel elementary, but they can actually provide significant introspection and discussion. No matter what a person's maturity or comfort level is, anybody can provide a numerical response. However, it forces someone to think specifically about their life. Once a person gives the simple numerical answer, they've spoken aloud and are therefore more likely to open up about their answer.

Remember to conclude with specific responses to your time of study. This week be sensitive yet vulnerable in sharing areas of suffering and faith.

Week 3: Spiritual Growth

Start by reviewing the previous group session and asking group members to share any insights or experiences related to the previous week's study. This step is important, so allow enough time to share and review, but be careful to protect the time needed to watch and discuss this week's video.

Based on what we've learned during the past week and in today's session, in what ways is Christ all-sufficient as the source of the Christian life?

This question highlights a theme of this study and a key trait in a relationship with Jesus. Despite suffering, struggles, or any circumstance we may face, He's all-sufficient in meeting every need in our lives.

Robby began this session by saying that Jesus' statement "I am the true vine" (John 15:1) means that He's our source. At the same time, He was making a connection that the disciples would have immediately recognized. By calling Himself the True Vine, He was explaining how He represents the completed version of the religious system of the day (see Isa. 5:1-7).

What's the difference between pruning and purging?

When have you experienced a painful season that you later recognized as pruning that resulted in fresh growth in your life?

What fruit have you seen from the pain and growth of pruning?

Pruning is cutting back something that's good on a branch so that even more fruit can come from it. An example of pruning might be cutting out something that's not necessarily bad from your life in order to focus more on something that's great.

Purging is getting rid of trash. A vinedresser of Jesus' day purged the weeds that cropped up around his vines so that they didn't choke it out. We need to entirely get rid of some things in our lives because they're filthy and actively hindering our spiritual growth.

> **How often do you excuse your lack of prayer, time alone with God, or worshiping Him because you're too busy?**

> **When do you spend time alone with the Father?**

> **What kinds of things do you pray for?**

Robby mentioned in the video that the busier Jesus was, the more He prayed. As you close, use the following four questions to discuss how your group prays. On inspection all believers can identify things they can do to improve their prayer lives.

Mark 1:35 says of Jesus, "Very early in the morning, while it was still dark, He got up, went out, and made His way to a deserted place. And He was praying there." Even on the heels of a long day and at the start of another one, Jesus made an extra effort to be alone with His Father.

> **What areas of your life do you need to rearrange in order to spend more time with God?**

Robby closed with this question. We are a busier society than perhaps any that has come before us, but the way we remain in Christ is to constantly connect with Him through prayer.

The closing prayer activity helps group members focus on the fact that God desires a relationship with us. An essential part of any relationship is communication—in this case, prayer.

Week 4: The Path to Life

Start by reviewing the previous group session and asking group members to share any insights or experiences related to the previous week's study. This step is important, so allow enough time to share and review, but be careful to protect the time needed to watch and discuss this week's video.

> **How did spending time in the Word this week adjust your focus on Jesus?**

You're now at the halfway point in the study. Use this question to remind everyone about the importance of God's Word in the life of a disciple.

> **What ways do people try to find God other than through Jesus?**

> **How does John 14:1-6 highlight the need for us to share the gospel?**

> **What excuses are made for being hesitant to share this gospel truth?**

Humanity has always wanted to elevate its ways above God's. Jesus flips the equation around. The things we contrive can never get us to God because they were built by human hands. Jesus is the way to the Father because He's the only One who has come from the Father in order to make a way. A right relationship with God is a matter of eternal life or death.

Be careful not to let the discussion be derailed by irrelevant philosophy, but rest in the truth of God's Word. At the same time, encourage different voices, for some have a perspective on this issue that can help others.

The final discussion questions direct the group's attention away from historical Jewish weddings and from speculation about how the disciples felt when hearing what Jesus said to them by focusing on what this Scripture means for believers today.

> If you took stock of your life right now, would you say you're living as if your Groom is coming back to get you?

> How is the knowledge that Jesus is the only way to the Father challenging, encouraging, or insightful for you?

As you conclude the group time with some personal questions and prayer, make an evangelistic appeal to your group. This is perhaps a good time to discuss how to share the gospel as well.

> Record areas of your life that aren't honoring God for the great price with which He bought you.

> Keep this list in mind as you go about your daily activities this week. Remember that as we live, we're also preparing ourselves for our Groom, who is coming back to get us.

When we understand the sacrifice Jesus made on our behalf, the way we live and the urgency with which we share the good news of the gospel will change. We'll recognize sin as a cheap imitation of the joy Jesus offers, and we'll recognize other people as valued by God.

Week 5: Experiencing the Kingdom

Start by reviewing the previous group session and asking group members to share any insights or experiences related to the previous week's study.

How did understanding the tremendous value your Heavenly Father sees in you affect the way you saw your life this past week?

It's important for group members to have a clear picture of Jesus as the exclusive way to know God before you study Nicodemus today.

Robby mentioned that Nicodemus's coming at night was significant in at least three ways.

A series of questions is provided to help group members recognize that this historic detail is also a symbolic reality that applies to their lives today.

What do you typically do to get answers to spiritual questions? What books or study tools have been helpful? To whom do you go with questions?

In what ways has this group been a safe place to ask honest questions? When was a time you had an honest question but were afraid to ask it in case someone overheard you? What was/is the question?

This week is intended for more personal discussion and testimonies. Take this opportunity in the study to dig deeper into what God is doing in people's lives.

If someone were writing your biography and wanted to include something that demonstrated your belief in Jesus, what do you think they would write?

This question is intended to help people think about their past, present, and future. When they have a picture of their lives in mind, the follow-up questions about personal testimonies and confession in prayer will flow more naturally.

Use the series of questions to help people talk through different aspects of their personal testimonies.

> **What did you first know about Jesus?**
>
> **How would you describe the lostness or darkness in your life before believing in Jesus?**
>
> **When were you born again?**
>
> **How has the new birth changed your life for the sake of God's kingdom?**

Be clear that as disciples, we should have answers to each of these questions. Refer back to the royal official and the group discussion in session 2. Remind everyone that James 2:14 says, "What good is it, my brothers, if someone says he has faith but does not have works? Can his faith save him?"

Reemphasize the fact that nothing has changed in the two thousand years since this conversation occurred. The kingdom of God is at hand, and we're each responsible for where we place our faith. Faith will change the way we live. The Bible reveals that Nicodemus placed true faith in Jesus, as shown by his participation in Jesus' burial after the crucifixion (see John 19:39).

During your time of prayer, group members will assess areas in which repentance is needed. It's vital that you model vulnerability and confession in this setting.

Week 6: Seeking in Our Doubt

Start by reviewing the previous group session and asking group members to share any insights or experiences related to the previous week's study. This step is important, so allow enough time to share and review, but be careful to protect the time needed to watch and discuss this week's video.

Robby talked about three different passages that mention Thomas. Before you begin your time of further study and discussion, you may want to ask three different people to look up the following passages: John 11:11-16; 14:1-7; 20:24-29.

Don't read all three stories at this time. Simply have people prepared to read them when each new story comes up during the discussion.

> **What preconceived ideas about Thomas did you have before hearing Robby's teaching?**
>
> **Did Robby's teaching change your opinion of Thomas? Why or why not?**

Remember that it's often helpful for a leader to start by asking questions that are broad enough to allow everyone to respond with their general reaction to the teaching but also specific enough to guide responses.

Now that people have begun to participate in discussion, move toward more personal experiences with the following questions.

> **When have you been hesitant to trust God? What kinds of excuses do you often offer for not doing what the Lord calls you to do?**
>
> **Is there anything you would be willing to die for? If so, what?**
>
> **How committed are you to the truth, even if it's difficult to hear?**

Help group members think about what they do to seek and discern truth. Challenge them to consider their openness to letting people speak the truth into their lives. Do they have a trusted friend who'll be completely honest in love, not just telling them what they want to hear?

Most of us say we're committed to the truth, but being willing to hear it, even when it challenges our beliefs, desires, or agendas is another thing.

As you move toward the conclusion of this Bible study, lead your group into a time of discussion that will reveal the reality of their faith in Jesus as the Son of God. Make yourself available for further discussion or explanation if you're comfortable doing so.

Using the final series of questions, encourage personal reflection, not only on ways we relate to Thomas but also on ways this Bible study has helped us know Jesus.

What proves to you that Jesus is who He says He is?

Would you consider yourself a passive believer or an active seeker of Jesus?

What about the account of Thomas quells a fear or doubt you have about who Jesus is?

What has been challenging, encouraging, or insightful from the case of the famous doubter Thomas?

Now that you've completed *Knowing Jesus*, determine what the group will study the next time you meet. Conclude the session with prayer.

Tips for Leading a Small Group

Prayerfully Prepare

Prepare for each group session with prayer. Ask the Holy Spirit to work through you and the group discussion as you point to Jesus each week through God's Word.

REVIEW the weekly material and group questions ahead of time.

PRAY for each person in the group.

Minimize Distractions

Do everything in your ability to help people focus on what's most important: connecting with God, with the Bible, and with one another. Create a comfortable environment. If group members are uncomfortable, they'll be distracted and therefore not engaged in the group experience. Take into consideration seating, temperature, lighting, refreshments, surrounding noise, and general cleanliness.

At best, thoughtfulness and hospitality show guests and group members they're welcome and valued in whatever environment you choose to gather. At worst, people may never notice your effort, but they're also not distracted.

Include Others

Your goal is to foster a community in which people are welcome just as they are but encouraged to grow spiritually. Always be aware of opportunities to include and invite.

INVITE new people to join your group.

INCLUDE anyone who visits the group.

Encourage Discussion

A good small-group experience has the following characteristics.

EVERYONE PARTICIPATES. Encourage everyone to ask questions, share responses, or read aloud.

NO ONE DOMINATES—NOT EVEN THE LEADER. Be sure your time speaking as a leader takes up less than half your time together as a group. Politely guide discussion if anyone dominates.

NOBODY IS RUSHED THROUGH QUESTIONS. Don't feel that a moment of silence is a bad thing. People often need time to think about their responses to questions they've just heard or to gain courage to share what God is stirring in their hearts.

INPUT IS AFFIRMED AND FOLLOWED UP. Make sure you point out something true or helpful in a response. Don't just move on. Build community with follow-up questions, asking how other people have experienced similar things or how a truth has shaped their understanding of God and the Scripture you're studying. People are less likely to speak up if they fear that you don't actually want to hear their answers or that you're looking for only a certain answer.

GOD AND HIS WORD ARE CENTRAL. Opinions and experiences can be helpful, but God has given us the truth. Trust Scripture to be the authority and God's Spirit to work in people's lives. You can't change anyone, but God can. Continually point people to the Word and to active steps of faith.

Keep Connecting

Think of ways to connect with group members during the week. Participation during the group session is always improved when members spend time connecting with one another outside the group sessions. The more people are comfortable with and involved in one another's lives, the more they'll look forward to being together. When people move beyond being friendly to truly being friends who form a community, they come to each session eager to engage instead of merely attending.

Encourage group members with thoughts, commitments, or questions from the session by connecting through emails, texts, and social media.

Build deeper friendships by planning or spontaneously inviting group members to join you outside your regularly scheduled group time for meals; fun activities; and projects around your home, church, or community.

Group Information

NAME   **CONTACT**

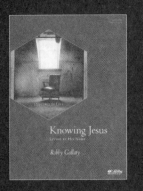

WHERE TO GO FROM HERE

We hope you enjoyed *Knowing Jesus*. If so, please share it on social media with #KnowingJesus. And now that you've completed this study, here are a few possible directions you can go for your next one.

UNDERSTANDING THE BIBLE

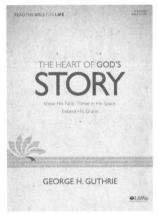

Discover the presence of God at the heart of His story, and understand why we were created, where we are heading, and how to live out the gospel in the world right now. (6 sessions)

UNDERSTANDING THE CHURCH

Gain a comprehensive and rich understanding of the church and the way its components work together for effective, transformative ministry. (6 sessions)

EVANGELISM

Discover the simple joy of evangelism as the good news of Jesus naturally overflows into your daily life. (6 sessions)